FRONT VE
BACK V.

Memories of a child of the

RAJ

by

ANNE GRIEGER

*I dedicate this book to my beloved parents,
Ena and Cyril; to my dear Ayah, Elizabeth;
and last but not least, to my much-loved sister,
Jane, whom we lost at the age of of fifty-five
to Multiple Sclerosis.*

Published privately in the United Kingdom in 2017
Copyright © 2017 Anne Grieger
Design Ginny Wood | gin.wood@sky.com

ISBN paperback 978-1-5272-1791-1

This paperback can be ordered from all bookstores as well as from eplatforms such as Amazon and Book Depository.

ACKNOWLEDGEMENTS

For all their assistance with the birth of this book, I would like to thank the following:

Brian Thompson and Gregory Caswell for their help and patient guidance when navigating the mysteries of my laptop.

Katie Isbester, Editor of Clapham Publishing Services, for her encouragement, help, and skilful editing.

Hamish, Ron and Tom for their advice on getting published.

My sister, Sue, for her input and encouragement; and my husband, John, for his advice and support.

Some photographs appear by Courtesy of 'The Hindu', India; of G.K. Vale & Co., Chennai, and of the former Gemini Film Studios, Chennai, where the picture on the back cover was taken.

The facts in this memoir are true to the best of my knowledge. I believe I have remembered correctly most of the names mentioned, but I have changed three surnames in order to protect the privacy of the people involved.

Finally, I want to thank India for giving me a delightful childhood, and so many happy memories.

Contents

CHAPTER ONE

Early Days

I have a birth certificate printed in Tamil as well as English. As a child of the British Raj, my birthplace in 1937 was the large and sprawling South Indian city of Madras, the capital of a Presidency with a British Governor. Though the State has long since been renamed Tamil Nadu, and the city, now Chennai, has developed enormously, they remain the heart of Dravidian India, with a pull as strong as any North West Frontier, Mogul palace or mighty river of Bengal. The numerous languages spoken in Southern India, such as Tamil, Telugu, Malayalam and Kannada, are known as Dravidian languages and thus give their name to this part of the country.

Though recent events involving the Tamil Tigers in Sri Lanka contradict this, South Indians are a gentle people. Perhaps they are conditioned by the fact that they have had to resist only the attacks of the British and not also those of the ferocious, marauding hordes of Moguls, as did their northern compatriots. The first South Indian I met was the gentlest and kindest of all I ever knew. My contact with her began in the first hours of my life. One might even say before that, for the night before I was born, she slept on the floor beside my mother's bed in the Lady Willingdon Nursing Home in Madras. My English parents had engaged her just that day because, when she came to offer her services as a nursemaid, they thought she had a kind face. She was my Ayah, Elizabeth, who loved and cared for me long past my childhood years, and whom I loved almost as my mother.

After a week, I was taken home to a bungalow that was not in fact a bungalow at all. It was a massive two-storied mansion called Wallace Gardens and my parents occupied the bottom half of it. The top storey was self-contained and lived in by a group of bachelors. Self-contained implies just two separate entrances, but this house had many doors leading out onto verandahs and used, at least on the ground floor, by a variety of God's creatures. These might include anything from innocuous beetles to a scorpion, snake, or even a mongoose. 'Poochies', as we children called the insects, were on the whole harmless, though we did sleep under mosquito nets and were taught, as we grew older, to shake out our shoes before we put them on. The story of the man who stepped into his shoes in the dark, and died from the sting of a scorpion lurking there, was one of the earliest tales we were told.

When I was eight months old my mother took me, her chubby first-born, 'home' to England to introduce me to my grandparents. We sailed from Cochin on a Bibby Line liner and with us came Ayah, who was to look after me while my mother enjoyed dinners and dances during the two-week voyage. Apparently, things did not work out that way. Ayah was sea-sick throughout and my mother ended up caring for both Ayah and the demands of a baby for the fortnight.

With my mother in the ship's canvas swimming pool, en route to
meet my grand-parents in England

Once in England, where we stayed with my maternal grandmother in Bedford, Ayah became her usual competent self. She took me to the park in my pram and was interrogated by the children there on why her skin was so black and why she wore such funny clothes. She told me many years later that she had marvelled at the cleanness and greenness of England and how lucky she was to have been there. Although it was summer, she did find it cold and needed a cardigan over her sari, but she took my grandmother's cooking in her stride. Being a Christian, she had no religious food requirements and ate roast beef and Yorkshire pudding with everybody else. In those days, there were no Indian restaurants in Bedford and I am sure there must have been times when she pined for a really chilli-hot curry. In all the thirty-five years my mother spent in South East Asia, she never managed to like curry and never ate it, so I am quite sure she could not cook one; and I doubt that Grandma would have let Ayah loose in her kitchen to do so, even if the ingredients for a vindaloo had been available

We spent four months in England and, much to Ayah's relief, returned to India on a larger, more stabilised liner of the P&O Line. My father had been unable to accompany us on this trip as he had to do a four-year stint and was not due 'home' leave until 1940. Because the war put paid to any voyages, this meant that he did not see 'home', the expatriate Englishman's term for Britain, for nine years.

Because of the rumblings about war in Europe, he was pleased to see us safely back in Madras, where we were joined a few months later by my mother's sister, Mary. My parents introduced her to all the bachelors they knew, and in the summer of 1939 she became engaged and married a rugby-playing teammate of my father's. The wedding took place at the oldest Anglican church in India, St. Mary's Church, Fort St. George.

More than any other place, Fort St. George with its 20-foot walls conjures pictures of the British in India. The fortress was finished in 1653 and was headquarters of the British East India Company, who opened a trading post in Madras long before they reached Bombay and Calcutta. The Fort played an important part in the British struggle for India and Robert Clive began his career there as a modest clerk in 1743. Only later did he achieve his spectacular successes as a military commander and subsequent elevation to Governor.

Madras has a Protestant cathedral, more modern and much bigger than the Fort church, but St. Mary's was the fashionable place for a Protestant wedding. On a visit to the church seventy-one years later, we were still able to see the record of my aunt's wedding in the Marriage Register and also, unearthed from an even more dilapidated ledger, the record of Clive's marriage in 1753.

I was, at nearly two, a bridesmaid at Aunt Mary's wedding. Attired in a frilly white dress and mob cap, I clung tightly to my mother's hand throughout. She was Matron of Honour and my father, a witness, gave the bride away at the ceremony.

I have no recollection of this occasion, but I have a vivid memory of an event that occurred a year later when I was three. I was waking up in the morning with my

Clinging to my mother's hand at Aunt Mary's wedding in Madras

eyelids stuck together – a case of conjunctivitis. Ayah had the remedy. She sat me on a chamber pot and held a piece of cotton wool under me while I peed. This she quickly applied, while still warm, to my eyelids. Whether or not I was cured I do not recall, and I doubt that my mother knew of the episode, but it certainly made a lasting impression on me.

This and other local customs and events coloured my childhood and made me grateful for the opportunity I had to witness life on both the front and back verandahs. I realise that this world is now gone, probably for the better. But I am also aware that people are curious and wish to know about this lost world. I have tried, as best I can, to share this lost world with the present day.

An Addition to the Family

When I was three, we moved from Wallace Gardens down Graemes Lane to Graemes Gardens. Like many of the old colonial houses, which were called bungalows, it had two storeys. We occupied the ground floor and on the floor above lived a couple with a young son, Tim, who was almost exactly my age. This was a bonus as it gave me an instantly available playmate and, as I later had only sisters, must have educated me in the tomboy ways of little boys. He and another boy, Patrick, also my age and the son of my mother's best friend, went with me to the swimming pool, to parties, and eventually to nursery school run by the mother of a fellow pupil at her bungalow.

Before this, however, my spoilt only-child existence was shattered by the arrival of my sister Jane. On a Sunday afternoon in November 1940, Ayah bundled me hurriedly into the car; I was told that I was going to play with Patrick. Fatty, our driver, took us to his bungalow, set in large gardens, where Patrick was nowhere to be found. He'd gone to Sunday school. I was kept amused for a while with his toys and then we drove home again. We were met on the front verandah by a nurse holding a tiny baby. I was told "Your little sister has arrived". As planned, she was born at home in Graemes Gardens and was named Sarah Jane.

I'd been warned for some time that I'd soon be getting a brother or sister. I don't remember being jealous, but I'm sure there must have been times when I resented the loss of my parents' full attention. Of course, I had my beloved Ayah, who also cosseted and cared for me. At this time I was given a baby doll, which closed its eyes when laid down and made a strange crying noise when tipped over. I spent the next few months busily administering comparable attention to it while I watched my baby sister being fed, burped and lulled to sleep. Any misgivings about having a younger sister were soon forgotten as Jane grew and became my endearing, and in later life, very much-missed, close companion.

At about this time, we were joined by Kanaan, our new bearer, who never left my parents through the many years they spent in India. He was a Hindu and in charge of the whole household, although he never managed to be in charge of Ayah. He always wore a white jacket and trousers and a white turban, and served us at the table.

From an early age, my mother took me to watch my father
playing cricket

He also meticulously laid out my father's clothes every morning and packed his sports gear for the clubs, where my father exercised most evenings. Later, when required, he would lay out black tie and dinner jacket, which was the usual wear for cocktail parties and evenings out.

Kanaan was married and lived with his wife and three children in a godown in the compound (garden). This was a small windowless room, open to the front, which was part of a stable block that had been built for the horses that drew the carriages of earlier members of the Raj. Some of the upstairs servants also had godowns there. Under the covered walk-way that fronted the length of the block, each occupant had now constructed a three-sided fireplace of bricks for cooking, so at least they did not have to endure smoke inside their sleeping quarters.

From left, Kanaan and the assistant bearer with a visiting playmate in front of the elephant porch at Graemes Gardens

The kitchen for our own household was almost as primitive. It was a small dark room with a range built from bricks and mud and stoked by charcoal. There was some sort of oven arrangement from which Cookie produced typical English dishes like roasts and toad-in-the-hole, and I still marvel now at how he managed it all. Not surprisingly, my mother, who was no cook, hardly ever went in there. The kitchen was off the back verandah, which was very much the servants' domain. There Munswami, our waterman, did the washing-up, our dhobi (laundryman) ironed our clothes, and our derzi (tailor) sometimes made us dresses.

From the front verandah, a dozen steps led down to the huge porch, built at the time when visitors arriving by elephant needed the great height to accommodate the howdah on its back. Here, my parents' visitors arrived by car and never rang a bell or knocked as the many doors into the house were open all day long. There was a third verandah at the side to which, in the Hot Weather, my parents' beds were moved to enable them to sleep better in the cooler night air. From here, anybody could have wandered into the bungalow and pilfered whatever they wanted, but it never happened. We felt extremely safe even though we did not have a chokidar (watchman) on the gate and our servants did not sleep in the house.

In South India, servants called their employers 'Madam' and 'Master' and not 'Sahib' and 'Memsahib' as they did in the north of the country. We children were 'Missie' and 'Little Master', so we were 'Anne Missie' and 'Jane Missie', and my sister Susan, when she came along, was 'Little Missie'.

We Missies were able to wander everywhere, even into the servants' godowns, and often spent our time round the back of the house, curious to know what was going on in the servants' domain.

Ayah ensures my safety on a Club party carousel

OF SNAKES AND SNAILS AND PUPPY DOGS' TAILS

"Let's go and play with Raju," was something I often said to my sister Jane.

Raju was the eight-year old son of Kanaan, our bearer, and lived with his parents and two siblings in the one-room godown in the compound. His mother cooked their meals on an open fireplace. There were two servants' lavatories, one for men and one for women, and most of the bathing and washing took place out of doors at taps placed at the back of the house.

Our compound was large with tall trees and at one side, scrubby bushes and long grass. There the servants' activities did not impinge on the immaculate lawns and flowerbeds out front. Even the odd cows, which were forbidden by my father, had been stealthily tethered behind the hedges and gone unnoticed for weeks at a time. There was always a lot more of interest going on at the back, which was why we went to play there as often as we could.

"You must be careful those children don't go native," an imperious burra-memsahib (senior executive's wife) had once told my mother after listening to our chatter. If 'little girls are made of sugar and spice and all things nice', we were not living up to expectations.

In front of the bungalow, we had a sandpit and a swing hanging from an old banyan tree. At the back I had discovered something much more satisfying, not to say useful, than making mud pies. At the age of five, I learned how to make cow-dung pats. Cow-dung was a great source of fuel for our servants. Any droppings, whether from the road or the compound, were taken up enthusiastically. Making mud pies has nothing on making cow-dung pats. First, you must mix in straw to get the right consistency, then roll a ball about the size of a large orange, flatten it and smack it hard against the wall so that it sticks there. Once the sun has dried it to a suitable state for burning, it just falls off by itself. The cow-dung pats themselves don't smell much once dried, but the smoke when they are burned can be very acrid. Kanaan's wife always used them and her son was my teacher. Jane was my assistant. Three years my junior, she always liked to do what I did.

"Don't get it on your sun-suit," I ordered her now, "or they might find out what we've been doing."

Neither parents, nor Ayah, had yet discovered our latest game, but I knew instinctively that it would become a forbidden activity. We were squatting on our haunches, and I was concentrating hard on achieving the perfect cow-dung pat. Suddenly Jane jumped up with a shriek.

"There's a snake," she shouted. "Look, there's a snake!"

We were working on the hard-baked ground in front of the godown, but to the left of us the scrubby grass parted as a large cobra slithered swiftly to a hiding place under a bush. "Appa, Appa," shouted Raju, running into the godown where his father was having his afternoon siesta.

Kanaan stumbled out into the bright light, picking up a long stout stick he kept near the godown's entrance. We pointed out the bush. Cautiously, Kanaan crept forward and, as he approached, the cobra unwound with a hiss, its long fangs darting from its oval flat head. Kanaan gave it a mighty whack and knocked it back. Before it could raise itself once more, Kanaan, lashed out again and again until, with a final shudder, it lay still on the ground.

"Oh, poor thing!" said Jane.

"Don't touch, Missie," ordered Kanaan. "You all very lucky children. Cobra's bite very dangerous — killing many people."

"What do we do now?" I asked.

"I'm taking to show my friend," he answered. "But very important now, Missies, you be very careful playing in the compound. When one cobra killed, second cobra always coming looking for its mate."

"Truly?" I asked in awe.

"Yes, very truly, Missie. Everybody must look out now for second cobra —without fail, he's coming searching for this one."

We hurried back into the house to tell my mother and Ayah the news.

Ayah was mindful of Kanaan's warnings. Every time we went to play in the sand-pit she insisted on approaching it first, clapping her hands as she did so. Ostentatiously she turned over every bucket and tin and threw out the snails.

In a few days, we'd forgotten the danger. There was always something else on our minds. Our dog, Lassie, had recently produced eight puppies. Their father was a Labrador, like our Lassie, and belonged to 'Uncle' Bill next door. The pariahs, or pi-dogs as we called them, had been successfully chased from our gate, where they appeared at regular intervals. We were taught never to pat a stray dog in case it had rabies and turned to bite us.

The puppies were black and golden, four boys and four girls. Lassie was very protective and was only slowly allowing us near enough to play with them. They seemed to be growing every day, becoming increasingly agile and captivating. We wanted to keep them all but were told we could have just one. The other seven would have to go.

"I've promised Uncle Bill one of the boys," said my mother. "We'll have to see who else wants one."

We took it upon ourselves to find owners who would love our puppies as we did. "Would you like one of our puppies?" we asked selected 'Uncles' and 'Aunts' who came to the house. We called all our parents' friends Uncle and Aunt though none of them really were. Uncle Bill chose Bouncer, the biggest and cheekiest of the eight. To our delight nobody seemed to want the weakest and shyest, who was our favourite.

"We're going to keep Minnie," we told our parents, "so don't tell anybody they can have her."

The weekend was approaching when the puppies would be taken away to their new homes. We decided to send them off with a Puja party. We didn't understand exactly what Puja was, but it seemed to be something all Hindus did when they were asking for a blessing from their gods. We certainly wanted the gods to smile on our puppies. Also, we remembered the fun we'd had at the time of the Pongal festival in mid-January. Two cows, which had been secretly tethered in the compound since the New Year, had had their horns painted; one red, one blue, one yellow and one green. Ribbons and bells had been tied to them and then Kanaan had chased them right round the bungalow in a complete circle. His children, along with Jane and I, had run, laughing and shouting, in their wake. We were not sure whether it was to bless the house, its inhabitants or the cows, but it had certainly caused a great deal of commotion.

I broached the subject now.

The cobra still on his mind, my father said, "You're not to chase those puppies anywhere — especially not through any long grass."

"Why don't you just have a tea party for them on the front lawn," suggested my mother. "You can ask Cookie to bake them some special biscuits."

"Alright," I said, "and we'll tie bows on their tails; pink for the girls and blue for the boys."

That afternoon, with the bows tied after some struggle, we shepherded the pups onto the close-cropped lawn. A table and chairs had been set out for our tea. Lassie was quite happy now to let her pups wander at will, and this they most certainly did. It was hard work making sure they did not go too far away while we set up saucers of weak tea and divided the biscuits. Bouncer was particularly inquisitive and we must have turned our backs on him for too long. Suddenly there was a loud yelping from the bushes near the compound wall.

"Oh my God!" exclaimed my father. "It's that snake. Stay where you are. I'll get him." He rushed over to Bouncer, grabbing his walking stick on the way. Kanaan followed him with a boulder in his hand. The puppy had stopped yelping. We waited in shocked silence. Then my father let out a laugh.

"It's all right, girls," he called to us. "Come and look."

We all crowded round. The blue-ribboned stump was wagging furiously as Bouncer stood proudly over his find: the decaying remains of a very large cobra.

"I'd say it's been killed by a mongoose some time ago." My father turned to Kanaan.

"Yes, Master — mongoose bitten through here."

Kanaan had taken the walking stick and was turning the snake over. "I telling you, Missies, second cobra always coming back. This must have been first cobra — other one second one."

By now, Jane was cuddling Bouncer in her arms. "You clever little puppy," she told him.

"You lucky little puppy," added my mother.

I pondered on Kanaan's wisdom — not only had he been right about the cobras, but also about doing Puja. It was obvious that the gods were smiling on us all.

CHAPTER TWO

KIDS IN THE COMPOUND

My sister Jane and I fell in love with them the day that they were born. They were two kids produced by Kamini. Kamini was the goat kept by our Ayah, who had scrimped and saved for months to buy her. Ayah considered her a commercial proposition because she produced milk not only for her ageing mother and herself, but also enough to sell to other servants.

Kamini's kids were the sweetest little things. When we saw them, not long after their birth, they could hardly stand and yet staggered to their mother to suckle.

"You can have them as pets," Ayah said. We were thrilled.

"Are they boys or girls?" we wanted to know.

"It's a pity, but only one is a girl," Ayah told us.

This surprised us. Our servants were usually more pleased to have a son, who would have greater earning capacity than a daughter. With goats it was different, Ayah explained. Nanny goats grew up to have kids and produce milk, while billy goats did nothing much. They just smelled.

"I like the little knobs on top of his head" I said. "I'll have him for mine and I'm going to call him Billie."

Jane thought for a moment, pushing her hand through her blonde fringe. "And I'll call mine Becky," said she, more imaginative than her older sister.

"But we'll have to make sure they're always tied up," Ayah told us. She was allowed to keep Kamini in the compound on the strict understanding that the goat was not allowed to wander freely. To come to this arrangement, Ayah had put in a special request on the grounds that Kamini's milk was good for her old mother, who was toothless and couldn't chew solids. Amma, the Tamil word for Mother and the name Jane and I used for her too, lived with Ayah in her godown. My mother, whose favourite of all the servants was Ayah, readily agreed. My father, who was keen on his garden, acquiesced reluctantly. Of all the servants his favourite was Kanaan, the bearer (butler/valet), usually summoned as 'Boy'! I have since come to realise that Dad and Kanaan understood each other perfectly.

In fact, it was Kanaan who gave me my first psychology lesson and it concerned my father. Dad was one of those people who lost his temper, erupted like a volcano and shouted at everybody in sight. Five minutes later the wrath was out of his system and he would forget all about it. After a particularly vituperative outpouring about something ridiculous like a sock with a hole in it, I was commiserating with Kanaan when he turned to me and said: "Missie — Master shouting, shouting, but not meaning."

It proved to be so time and time again.

It was the custom to take little masters and missies for at least one, and sometimes two, daily walks. The first came before breakfast, when the sun had not been up long enough to make the heat unbearable, though we were still made to wear topis or sun hats. The second was in the late afternoon, when the sun was going down and the day cooling off. At about 4 o'clock we were dressed in clean clothes and usually had tea with my mother. After that, we were taken off by Ayah in her spotless white sari to one of the local venues, where the children met to play, and the Ayahs and Nannies to gossip.

Patrick with his Nanny, and me with my Ayah, Elizabeth

Even as a child, I sensed that the nannies considered themselves superior to the ayahs. A nanny was what we called a nursemaid who was Anglo-Indian or of mixed blood, and almost always a Christian. She always wore white dresses. In the south, ayahs were usually Hindus, although one did find the occasional Muslim. Our Ayah was unusual in that she was a Catholic, and she had been to England. If the nannies considered her a lesser mortal, it made no difference to us. Jane and I would not have swapped Ayah for all the nannies on the sub-continent, or for that matter, for any in Kensington Gardens. Nursemaids in Britain had an easy time compared to ours, who always had to keep a very close eye on little masters and missies. There was no knowing what small inquisitive fingers would unearth from under stones or disturb behind bushes, where a scurrying scorpion or hissing cobra could bring death to their precious charges.

One afternoon, we were late setting off for our walk. Ayah had had trouble milking Kamini, whose yield was going down because Billie and Becky were too greedy. As we left, Ayah called to old Amma: "Make sure you tie Kamini up far enough away so that those two can't reach her."

We demurred. "They'll be hungry," said Jane.

"They are quite old enough to be eating more grass now," said Ayah in her 'no-nonsense' voice. We knew that tone from the times we had refused to eat prunes.

Because we were late, Ayah decided we would only go up the lane to the Rajah's compound. She had permission from the Rajah's servants to take us there to play. The Rajah himself — a minor potentate — was rarely in residence as he had several other properties dotted around the country that he used more frequently. In any case, the compound was so enormous that we could still have been in parts of it without anybody in the house knowing we were there.

Jane and I liked to wander around the flowerbeds

asking questions of the malis (gardeners). There were at least half-a-dozen of them watering the plants at this time of the evening, as indeed they were every evening, except at monsoon time. All over Madras at this time, the malis in the compounds of large houses would be watering their domains. At home, we had just one mali and a boy to help him. The Rajah did things on a much grander scale. "Woosh" went the water as the gardeners lifted the urns from their heads and sloshed their contents into the flowerbeds. The smell of warm drenched earth filled our nostrils. The malis turned on their bare heels and went back to the tank to fill up again. Their lungis (loincloths) were folded up around their thighs to keep them out of the wet. The only other cloth they wore was around their heads. Soft and often brightly coloured, this was wound in a special way to leave a flat platform on top. Then it was easy to balance the watering pot, which was either of metal or clay.

By going-home time we'd caught a frog. It had swooshed out of a pot with the water and rapidly managed to disturb the pristine freshness in which we had set out. Tired and happy, we wended our way back to discover our own mali in a state of hysteria.

"Look, look," he shouted at Ayah in Tamil the moment he caught sight of her. "Look what your goats have done to my flowers."

We looked, aghast. The flowerbed nearest the house had been partially flattened. Any plants left standing had been deheaded. The bright scarlet petals of the cannas, my father's pride and joy, lay scattered on the ground. A great deal of greenery had been munched. Somebody had had a feast.

"Just wait till Master sees all this," babbled Mali. "He'll be furious. He'll get rid of your silly goats if he doesn't get rid of you!" Mali was right to be worried. There were many Indians and few had as good a job as he did. I'm not saying that was right, I'm just saying that that was the way it was back in those days.

"Oh dear God," wailed Ayah equally concerned about her employment, "what am I going to do? Have you tied them up again? Where are they?" and she rushed off to look for the culprits.

"Perhaps it'll be dark before Dad comes home," I ventured to Jane.

"Here he comes now," was her reply as the car turned into the gateway at the end of the drive. My father had come straight home from the office and not gone to play tennis at the club as he sometimes did. Tired and crumpled after a hot, sticky day, he jumped out of the car and came towards us.

"Hello girls, what are you up to?" and then, taking in the destruction, "What the bloody hell has been going on here? I know — it's those bloody goats! Just let me get my hands on them! I'll wring their necks! Where's that damned woman — Ayah!"

There was silence. We knew that Mali was inwardly giving thanks to his gods that his neck appeared to be escaping the danger.

"Ayah!" my father bellowed again.

Suddenly a voice piped up. It was Jane Missie.

"It wasn't her fault, Daddy," she said. "Billie and Becky were jumping around and hurting their necks, so I undid their ropes."

My father looked at her for a long moment.

"Huh," he said. There was a long pause. "That was a silly thing to do."

He turned and stomped into the house to find my mother. Jane and I looked at each other — and grinned. We knew that'd be the end of the matter. Old Amma could have her milk, Ayah could still make extra money and, best of all, we'd still have Billie and Becky as pets.

MONKEY BUSINESS

Still wearing my nightie, I leaned over the parapet wall and watched Ayah at the tap below. Ayah was performing her morning ablutions. Her face she washed as we would, swilling water over it and patting it dry with the end of her sari. What interested me was the way she cleaned her teeth. As a toothbrush, Ayah used the forefinger of her right hand, as toothpaste, crumbled charcoal. The paste this made when mixed with water was rubbed around her teeth and mouth. I couldn't understand how such a horrible black mess produced such sparkling white teeth. Anyway, it looked like fun. To rinse the mess away, Ayah carried the water from tap to mouth in her cupped hand. That's a habit I picked up then and have kept all my life — though in India we were never supposed to drink water direct from the taps. Water for drinking was always boiled and kept in bottles in the fridge. Tap water was strictly forbidden, and so was charcoal as toothpaste. This morning I begged again:

"Ayah, let me try some — please."

Ayah shook her head in the way that meant 'No'. Sometimes Indians shake their heads in agreement, but that's a slow movement from side to side. This was a definite 'No'.

"Missie, you know Madam wouldn't like it," she said. "Now go back to the bathroom and clean your teeth with the proper toothpaste. In a minute I'll come and call Munswami to bring your bath water."

Although our bathrooms had running water, it was only cold water. Hot water had to be heated in large cauldrons on charcoal braziers near the back verandah. In the Cold Weather, from November to February, we had warm baths. In the Hot Weather it was a relief to get into water as cold as we could make it. Then we ran the water from the tap and let it stand for hours in the cool bathroom. Now, in the Cold Weather, the temperature was only reaching 84*F at the hottest time of the day, so Munswami, our waterman, had to carry in the heavy pans and pour the hot water into our baths. It was not his only duty. He also did the washing-up and peeled the vegetables for Cookie. Sometimes he kept an eye on us for Ayah. He was in fact the household's general dogsbody: always around but not much noticed.

On my way back to the bathroom I passed our bearer Kanaan, who headed the servant hierarchy. At least that's what he thought, though I knew Ayah had different ideas.

"Good morning Missie," he smiled.

I closed my lips in a straight line and went by without a word. I wasn't speaking to Kanaan; in fact I was furious with Kanaan, who had had the cheek to accuse my Ayah of stealing. Apart from the few times I'd forgotten, I hadn't said a word to him in the last four days. Except of course to call him a 'Korungu' (a monkey), which was the rudest word I knew in Tamil. I had flung that at him during one of the heated exchanges he and Ayah kept having about the missing stores. These were the dry groceries like sugar, flour and rice, quantities of which had been mysteriously disappearing for a fortnight.

I went into the bathroom and reached for my blue toothbrush and the boring tube of toothpaste. My sister Jane came running in from my parents' bedroom. When Kanaan took them their early morning tea, she liked to go and climb into their bed.

"Did you remember not to talk to Kanaan?" I asked sternly.

As Janie was three years my junior, she was not very good at keeping up feuds. She was very fond of Kanaan — as I was if I had to admit it. He had told us stories, played games and amused us for hours on the occasions when Ayah had a day off and my parents had to go out. But if it came to a fight, there was no question whose side I would be on — just as I knew Ayah would stick by me through thick and thin. She came in now muttering something about that 'cunning Hindu'. In situations like this, the question of religion always came to the fore. Ayah was a Catholic and, except for Joseph, one of our two drivers, the other servants were all Hindus. The idea that she, educated by missionaries, would ever steal anything was inconceivable; to her, to me, and also to my mother. But here was Kanaan insisting that it must be she who had raided the store cupboard; she was the only one who'd dare. The feud was disrupting the harmony of our household, and my father had begun making rumbling noises about 'somebody having to go'.

Munswami came in with the hot water. Usually he was full of chatter, telling Ayah about his children, and his wife who had just had yet another baby. He did not live in the compound because there was not enough room, but came from the cluster of mud huts down at the end of our lane. Today he was very quiet and had, I assumed, lined up on Kanaan's side. Not that this was surprising. Apart from being a Hindu, although of a lower caste, he often ran errands for Kanaan, who usually let him take the leftovers from our meals.

My mother also handed out food. In addition to their salaries, she gave each servant a quantity of dry stores at the beginning of each month. So she couldn't understand why some should be missing from our own store cupboard. This was a wooden contraption with a wire-netting door. Like the fridge, it stood with its feet in small tins of kerosene to stop the ants climbing up for anything sweet. This was not as dangerous as it sounds in the case of the refrigerator because it ran on kerosene not electricity. Kanaan kept the store cupboard locked. This didn't concern us children because the fridge, where the fizzy drinks and chocolate were kept, was usually our goal. Anyway, we knew in which tin on the pantry shelf he kept the store cupboard key — as probably did everybody else. But the question of who was using it was upsetting us all.

It made me restless. We were supposed to lie on our

beds after lunch, while the servants had their midday meal.

"I'm going to see if Mummy is awake," I said.

Jane climbed off the bed to follow me.

"You're not to wake her up if she's sleeping," ordered the bossy elder sister.

We tip-toed across the dining room. Passing the pantry I heard a rustle. I caught my breath. I knew there shouldn't be anybody there at this time. I motioned to Jane to stand back and peered around the door. Munswami stood at the table pouring rice into the cloth he normally wore as a turban.

"Get Mummy," I whispered to Jane. I marched in and demanded: "What are you doing Munswami?" He spun round, startled.

"Missie, please don't tell Master. He's getting very angry and my baby is sick and the children — they not getting enough to eat."

My mother arrived on the scene.

"Anne, you'd better call Kanaan," she said. "I want to hear what all this is about".

So the story came out. Munswami's baby was in hospital and he couldn't afford to pay for the medicine and food for his children. So he had hoped that nobody would notice if he helped himself from the store cupboard.

"Why didn't you come to me straight away?" asked my mother.

In Tamil, a torrent of words tumbled out. Kanaan translated. "Master has already given him an advance on salary and he dare not ask for any more." Finally they sorted it out. Munswami vowed that he would never take anything again. My mother would forget about the first advance and give him another one, which he could pay back over several months. She would also pay for the baby's medicine.

My father was always saying that the servants all knew how to get round Madam, but I think she could tell a sob story from a true one. I believed this was a true one, just as I'd believed that my Ayah would never steal. Vindicated, I turned to Kanaan now.

"You see, I told you Ayah wasn't a thief."

Then, with all the graciousness a five-year old could muster, "and you're not a Korungu either," I added, as he locked up his precious store cupboard. He said nothing and we only discovered months later the new hiding place for the key.

THE MISSING LINKS

"It must be that damned Munswami," insisted my father for the umpteenth time. "I bet he's in debt again and has flogged them in the bazaar. I've looked everywhere for them. If they were anywhere in the house, one of us would have found them by now."

That was true, I thought, standing patiently while my mother plaited my chestnut pigtails. We had all, even three-year old Jane, searched high and low for Dad's cufflinks.

My sister Jane and me, with my mother, en route to a Fancy
Dress party

They were the gold ones his mother had given him when he left England for his first tour of duty in the East. We knew how much he treasured them, especially as Granny was no longer alive to give him presents.

"I want to hand them down as a family heirloom," he'd said, looking at Jane and me. "Even if you don't have any brothers, one of you is bound to have a son to pass them on to."

"I'm quite sure Munswami wouldn't have taken them," responded my mother. "Not after the last time." Munswami, our waterman, who had been caught stealing food for his children from the store cupboard, had promised never to do it again and my mother believed in him.

"I'm going to tackle him about it," said my father, "and if I think he's taken them, then he'll have to go."

"Let's wait till Kanaan gets back at least," was my mother's answer.

"If Kanaan hadn't gone away to that blasted wedding, I'd never have lost them," grumbled my father illogically. "Anyway, I know I haven't lost them. They wouldn't just fall out by themselves".

"Perhaps a monkey came and took them," Jane piped up.

Fair-haired, like our mother, she was also already learning our mother's aptitude for pouring oil on troubled waters. Besides, it wasn't such a crazy idea. Monkeys had been known to come into houses to steal fruit if it was left lying about. It had never happened in our house, but I had seen a monkey darting away with a banana from a bowl of fruit in somebody else's dining room.

"Yes, I know which two-legged monkey that was," snorted Dad. "Muthu should have taken better care of them."

Muthu was the assistant bearer, who was standing in for Kanaan as my father's valet. He was very young and not yet well trained by Kanaan. Fortunately, his valeting duties only involved putting away and laying out the clothes for Master to step into. All the washing and ironing was done by a dhobi.

Our dhobi came once a week to do the washing for the whole family. He stayed all day and took over the spare room bathroom, which always gave the impression of being totally awash all morning. There was water everywhere as he scrubbed and beat the heavier items on the tiled floor. This of course was no substitute for the rocks he would have used in the river at Guindy, had he taken our clothes away. Though they received less of a beating, our clothes were probably cleaner than those washed in the not too clean river water at Dhobipet. They probably also lasted longer.

However, we children did regret one thing. As the dhobi didn't take our clothes away, there was no need for him to bring his donkey. Like most dhobis, he owned one to carry his loads. Sometimes though, he collected somebody else's washing on his way to us. Then we saw how the poor creature carried two enormous bundles, usually tied in sheets, and slung across its back so that a load hung at each flank. Jane and I made sure the bundles came off while the poor animal was with us for the day, and that she was tied in a good place to graze — not of course near father's flowerbeds. We saw that she had shade as well as food, though she didn't seem to mind the pounding of the mid-day sun.

The dhobi had come this morning — with his donkey, which was carrying no loads. We were surprised.

"Have you just brought her for a walk?" asked Jane.

"No Missie. Kirby Madam not giving me any clothes for washing this week because one of Master's shirts is lost. I think somebody stolen it from my line in Dhobipet. I'm not finding it anywhere. Some people very bad, Missie. If no washing, then no money."

I wondered about the bad people. Did he mean Mrs. Kirby or the thief? Dhobi started sorting our clothes into piles. He always washed the heavier things first so that they would be dry by lunchtime. Almost everything, with the exception of a few items that Madam warned him would fade in the hot sun, was hung outside to dry. The more fragile articles hung in the shade on the long back verandah.

Jane and I liked dhobi days because, in the afternoon, when we were supposed to be resting, we would creep out to the back verandah to watch our dhobi ironing and to hear stories about the other households he washed for. Today we had some news for him: the story of the missing cuff-links.

"I think a little boy with grease all over him came and stole them in the night," I ventured. This idea appealed to my six-year old imagination and was the result of warnings that Ayah had given us. According to her, small boys were sometimes used as thieves because they could squeeze through the iron bars that protected the windows of many houses. To enable them to do this, they worked completely naked and were covered from head to toe in coconut oil. Then, if anybody did catch them, they were slippery enough to wriggle free and run away. As my parents always slept with the doors of their bedroom wide open to the side verandah, there would have been little need for squeezing through iron bars; I could see I was impressing Jane with the story, if not the dhobi. He smiled and carried on placidly with the ironing.

To practise this fine art he stood at a heavy wooden table covered with an old blanket and a piece of clean white sheeting. I call it an art because he ironed everything from the flimsiest voile nighties to the linen sheets with the same massive iron completely independent of any power supply. Inside it, he coaxed lumps of charcoal to a red-hot intensity. The iron was too heavy for Jane and me to lift, but he wielded it as a craftsman. To test its temperature he would throw water on the sole plate, which made the drops sizzle and jump off in an alarming way. He seemed to know exactly how much sizzle he needed for any particular fabric.

Now he picked up a pair of the white drill trousers my father wore to the office every day. He laid them on the table and smoothed his hand across in preparation for the heavy iron. He stopped, puzzled, at a bump just below the waistband in front. All my father's trousers were made with a little pocket there for small change. Our dhobi undid the button and pulled out some soggy paper. Wrapped inside were the missing cufflinks.

"Oh Dhobi," I cried, "Daddy will be so pleased." I seized the would-be heirloom and rushed to my mother.

"Look Mummy! Look at what the dhobi's found in Daddy's trousers. Please ring him up and ask if we can give Dhobi a reward."

I had recently been read a story about a small boy who was given a reward for handing in a wallet he had found. Then I told her about Mr. Kirby's shirt and 'no work, no money'.

"We'll see," she said, dialling the office.

When my father heard, his first reaction was horror. "My God, they could have been crushed by that iron. I'm surprised they are not broken from the washing. But I remember now," Dad told my mother. "I wrapped them up in a piece of paper and put them in that pocket when I had to roll up my sleeves the other day. Kanaan would have found them of course, but you had better give the dhobi 10 rupees. After all, he could have hung on to them and we'd have been none the wiser."

The dhobi was summoned and given his reward with Master's special thanks. His surprise and delight were a pleasure to see. Jane jumped up and down with the excitement of it all. Little did she know that she too would be a link in this story. Although we had another sister, we never did have a brother, and it was Janie who bore the first son.

The Tamarind Tree

Going to the Madras Cricket Club, or 'Chepauk' as it was known, was fun for us children. As at most of the clubs, there were swings, slides and see-saws to keep us happy. At the Cricket Club, there was even a climbing frame, which we loved to assault, sometimes bunching up our dresses inside our knickers to make somersaults and other manoeuvres easier. We'd hang upside-down from the highest bar as Ayah, watching our faces turn from pink to puce, pleaded, "Now come down Missies, come down at once."

On Sunday mornings, when there was a cricket match, the chairs were set in rows on the club lawn. Members would sit there under the trees downing cold beers and then, as lunchtime approached, pink gins. I rarely remember anyone being drunk, although I suppose they must have been given the sheer volume of alcohol consumed. But either it was sweated out or the English had stronger constitutions in those days because language was never slurred and no one ever stumbled.

We children ran around on the boundary, hoping the ball would come our way and saying, "My Daddy's going to make a hundred today." To Jane's and my delight, ours quite frequently did. My mother usually took her knitting and was often chided for not paying attention. Either my father had hit a six or had been clean bowled at precisely the moment she was picking up a dropped stitch or intently casting on.

After the match had finished, we were allowed to 'help' Ramaswami, the grounds-man, pull out the little flag posts marking the boundary. The wicket itself was hallowed ground and only he was allowed to draw out the stumps. But we loved to run all round the edge of the pitch, competing to pull out the most flags. On the side furthest from the clubhouse, tall trees overlooked the grounds. Into these the local lads would climb, like monkeys in clusters, to get a grand-stand view of the game. Years later, when the authorities wanted to make the grounds into an official stadium, it was made known through Ramaswami how much the locals objected to losing their grand-stand seats. The year the stands were completed, my father happened to be President of the Club. He decided that any small boys particularly keen to watch the minor cricket matches should be allowed in free if they sat quietly on the far boundary line.

Now this same cricket pitch is the M.A. Chidambaram Stadium, where Test Matches are played when teams from different countries visit Madras (Chennai). The Club, much modernised, still sits beside the cricket field and members are given a splendid view of the play. The enormous public stands, which have been built around the remainder of the pitch, have changed the venue beyond recognition.

Originally, in the Club's grounds there grew an old Tamarind tree, whose pods Ayah liked to collect. On one occasion, when she was not with us, we managed to upset one of the Club's most venerable members. He was a crusty old burra-sahib, whose wife had long since given up both on him and on India, and had taken their two young sons 'home' to England. He lived at the Club in one of the suites available for single members. Younger expatriate bachelors in India very often shared a house. This arrangement was known as a 'chummery', but most clubs had some living quarters and Cuthbert had lived on his own at the Cricket Club for years. He considered it virtually 'his property', so when he found Jane and me throwing up sticks into the

Tamarind tree, he nearly exploded with rage.

"And what do you think you're doing?" he roared at us. Without waiting for an answer, he took each of us by the shoulder and marched us back to our parents on the lawn.

"I found these two scallywags trying to break up the Tamarind tree," he exaggerated.

"We weren't!" I protested indignantly.

"No," Jane continued. "We were only trying to get some pods for Ayah."

"Whatever for?" asked my father.

"She soaks them in water, squeezes them and then uses the drained liquid for her curry," I told him.

My mother smiled sweetly at the old boy.

"You see, Cuthbert," she said, "they really didn't mean to damage the tree and," here she turned to us, "they won't do it again, will you girls?"

"No, next time we'll get one of the ball-boys to climb up and pick them," said Jane earnestly.

Hurriedly my father intervened. "Let me buy you a drink, Cuthbert," and he shepherded him off to the Men Only bar, which was an institution favoured by most of the clubs formed by the British in India.

This bar was in full view of the lawn where my mother was sitting, and where most of the wives chose to congregate rather than in the somewhat pokey lounge allowed to them. Sometimes, when they grew tired of waiting for their menfolk to take them home, they would summon a peon (club servant) and send a chit (note) to their husbands — only a few yards away — requesting their immediate return. More often than not the reply came back by word of mouth,

"Master sending salaams and another whiskey-soda for Madam."

Admittedly, the men were probably thirsty because they had been playing tennis, squash or hockey, all of which were possible at the Cricket Club, but their wives did not appreciate this generosity.

The Club had six tennis courts and two squash courts, where my father played often. He was good at both games and the next afternoon was due to play in the final of a squash tournament. Kanaan packed his gear and my mother, Jane and I took it to meet him at the Cricket Club after work. Normally we would have hung over the squash court wall to watch his efforts, but while my mother did just that, we wandered off. Today we had another agenda: the gathering of Tamarind pods, and for that we needed a ball-boy.

The ball-boys taken on at the Club were all very keen to become excellent tennis players. If one of them was good enough he could hold the coveted position of No. 1 Marker. The Marker's job was to play with any member who needed a partner, whether novice or player good enough to represent his country. Our Marker had the ability to encourage and bring out the best in the most timid of players. I have seen him patiently lob ball after ball across the net to a spot the beginner could just reach if he moved fast enough. He was a superb player and could beat just about every member of the Club. He presided over his tennis courts and an army of ball-boys, whom he drilled, with immense pride.

So the ball-boys practised whenever they could,

mostly on the end court, which was usually empty. Jane and I made our way there and found two boys hitting a ball back and forth.

"We need you to help us," I said, and led the way to the Tamarind tree. "Please climb up and pick us some pods." It was an order, not a request. Although I was six years old and the ball-boys were all youngsters verging on adulthood, I was in charge and we all knew it.

"Missie, Master getting very angry if we do that," replied one of the boys.

"Just shake a branch then," I told him, "and they will fall down."

He climbed the tree and began shaking it. Suddenly a voice thundered behind us.

"And what do you think you are doing?"

It was 'Uncle' Cuthbert. The ball-boy clambered down and explained what had happened.

"I'll talk to you later," he told him, and led us back to the lawn, where my father was recovering after winning his squash match.

"You need to keep these girls under control," he told my mother sternly. "Where's their ayah?"

"She didn't come with us today," replied my mother. "Why, what have they done?"

"They were encouraging the ball-boys to break up the Tamarind tree again, and I've a good mind to have those boys sacked" he raged.

"Oh Cuthbert, isn't that a bit harsh? You wouldn't want your boys' careers blighted for such a small misdemeanour, would you?" responded my mother.

"I will certainly give them a good rocket," retorted Cuthbert, and then after a pause, "and I suppose it was your girls who led them astray." He stomped off. The minute he was out of sight, we ran back and picked up the fallen Tamarind pods.

BIRTHDAY WISHES

That day, my seventh birthday, dawn was just breaking when I woke. Ayah was still asleep on the floor beside my bed. Normally, by the time I opened my eyes, she had gone to make the strong black coffee she always drank first thing in the morning. But today was different. Today I couldn't sleep. It wasn't just that it was my birthday or that we were having a party. Far more exciting than that! The party we were having would have a conjurer and a merry-go-round, our very own carousel erected in the garden. The men would be coming soon to put it up, and I wasn't going to miss a moment of it. Jane was still asleep in the bed the other side of me. I pushed up the mosquito net and climbed carefully over Ayah. She woke with a jerk and sat bolt upright, alert as usual to the slightest movement of her sleeping charges.

"It's alright Ayah. I just want to see if the merry-go-round men have come yet."

I padded over the cool marble floor to the window. Like all the bungalow's windows, it was barred to stop intruders but had no glass. I pushed aside the voile curtains and peered out at a compound shrouded in semi-darkness.

The sun was just visible and the air, still cool, gave little indication of the humid heat it would carry later in the day.

"Missie, nobody's coming so early. Go back to sleep now, there's a good girl."

Ayah had rolled up her mat and was winding her sari around the long waist petticoat and bodice she wore as night clothes. She came over and kissed my cheek.

"Happy Birthday Anne Missie," she said gently. "I hope you will always have happy birthdays. Now I'm going to have my coffee and, when I come back, you can have your bath."

"Happy Birthday, Happy Birthday," called Jane from the bed. " What's happening? Can you see anything?"

"It's too early, Missie," Ayah explained. "Nothing will happen until after breakfast. First we'll go for a walk and then, after breakfast, there may be something to watch."

In fact it was during breakfast that we heard the hand-carts scrunching up the drive and the men calling to each other as they dragged the heavy wooden parts of the merry-go-round into the compound. We ran outside, begging Dad and our bearer Kanaan to come at once to make sure the men knew where to put everything.

The round-about was to go in the middle of the lawn. A hole would have to be dug to take the main central support. This desecration of his garden would not be enjoyed by my father. Fortunately, it wasn't every birthday that warranted a merry-go-round. But this was to be my last before I was packed off to school in England, so my parents had decided to make it one I would remember. There was always a carousel at the children's Christmas parties held at the various clubs, but not everybody had one for a party in their own garden.

The other entertainment was to be the Magic Man or conjuror. I had chosen him in preference to a Punch and Judy show or the Snake Charmer. The decision hadn't been easy. The Snake Charmer's cobra lent a certain excitement to any proceedings as he swayed to his master's flute and darted his tongue at the surrounding circle of children. If he was made to fight a mongoose, we held our breath in anticipation; but the cruel end we awaited was always averted and both participants lived to fight — and earn — another day.

Watching a performance by the Magic Man:
myself, Patrick, Diane, Tim in front

The Magic Man performed conjuring tricks that made us laugh and wonder, but it was his grand finale that intrigued me. He would make his wife climb into a large box-shaped basket, close the lid on her, and then plunge his two-foot bladed knife into her several times. It amazed me that no blood was ever spilled and the poor woman always emerged, cowed but in one piece. I had seen the trick done often and I still didn't know the answer. Now I asked my father, "When will the Magic Man come?"

"After lunch I should think," was his reply. "And if you and Jane are going to stay out here watching, mind you put your topis (pith helmets) on. Uncle George may bring Marietta over shortly." Uncle George was my mother's brother who, with his wife and children, was on leave in Madras from his regiment stationed on the North West Frontier.

We wandered among the painted horses and gaudy carriages that would hang under the red and green striped canopy. The men worked hard putting up the main structure. Occasionally they would undo the soft colourful clothes they had wound as turbans and mop the sweat from their faces. Their banging and shouting brought the servants' children from their godowns. With dark, kohl-ringed eyes, they peered from behind bushes in curiosity and wonderment. We beckoned them closer and explained. Slowly, the merry-go-round was taking shape. The proud horses with flaring nostrils were hung in place on the outside. Closer to the centre, where the men would stand to turn the handles, were the carriages, shaped as cars or boats, for younger children too scared to sit astride a horse. Finally, the top canopy went on and all was ready.

"Give us a ride, give us a ride!" we begged, jumping up and down. Jane climbed into a carriage. Cousin Marietta and I chose horses on opposite sides. The servants' children stood wistfully by.

"Come on," I called, "you too."

"What will Master say?" asked Kanaan's eldest son, Raju.

"I'll tell him I asked you. It's my birthday," I said.

Jane beckoned to Raju. "Put little Meena in here with me."

Meena, Kanaan's youngest, was eighteen months old and wore nothing but a string around her plump stomach. The children climbed eagerly aboard. Two of the men stood at the centre shaft, ready to turn the handles that would set the round-about in motion. I don't know whether they had ever propelled such a motley load. The parents of my friends coming to the party would certainly have raised their eyebrows and feared what their little darlings might pick up from such company.

"We're ready now. Let's go!" I commanded. We moved off slowly and sedately.

"More, more," we called to the men and, as we gathered momentum, the exhilaration grew. Sweat streamed down the men's torsos, turning them still darker as they toiled.

"Faster, faster," shouted Marietta and I as our horses swung almost horizontal.

We had ridden merry-go-rounds before but never like this. The men bent to their work, laughing at our excitement.

It was Jane who finally shouted "Stop". Little Meena was about to be sick in the bottom of the carriage. Luckily, just then Kanaan came out to call us for lunch and was able to return her to the safety of her mother's lap.

After lunch on normal days we were supposed to rest. Today the household was far too busy for anything like that. Kanaan was cutting sandwiches, while Cookie organised jellies and cakes. My mother had the chokra, Kanaan's deputy, moving the dining room furniture. Ayah was hunting for little Missies, who had disappeared while she laid out the party clothes.

She found us in the compound near the servants' quarters. We had received word from the children there that the Magic Man had arrived. With him were his bundle of props, a large wicker basket and the compliant wife. We listened hard to the conversation, hoping to learn some tricks of his trade. He was giving nothing away, but he did want to know where he could leave his things while he and his wife went down to the bazaar for something to eat.

"He could put them on the back verandah," I mentioned casually, as Ayah led us away.

"You can have a bath now," she told us. "Then I will get ready, and you can put your dresses on at the last minute." The organdie party frocks hung ironed and waiting, as though standing to attention on their own. "I don't want you creasing them up before the guests come at 4 o'clock." It didn't occur to us then, but Ayah, in her best white sari, would also be receiving guests. Each Little Master and Missie would be accompanied by his or her ayah or nanny and, for the sake of the household, a good impression must be made.

We sat on the bed in our petticoats, knowing exactly how long it would take for Ayah to reach her godown.

"I'll go and see if it's there," I whispered to Jane.

"I'm coming too," she said, and we slipped out of the bathroom door onto the back verandah. And there, up at the far end, it stood — the Magic Man's big wicker basket, about 4 feet high and 3 feet square. Gingerly we lifted the lid and peered inside.

"It has a partition," I told Jane. "I suppose she gets in there and he sticks his knife in the other bit."

"But it's so small," she whispered back. "Much less than half."

"I wonder if I could fit inside." I started to climb.

"No don't," said Jane. "We'd better go back now."

But it was too late. I had scrambled over the edge and fallen into the basket.

"You're in the big bit," ventured Jane, "the part he puts his knife in. Oh do come out."

I tried, scratching my legs on the wicker as I endeavoured to pull myself over the side.

"It's too tall," I complained. "You'll have to pull me out."

But I knew it was too much to ask of a four-year-old. I let go of her hand and fell back inside.

"You'll have to fetch Ayah," I finally admitted.

"She'll be so cross." Jane answered.

"I know, but the Magic Man will be even crosser if he finds us here. Hurry up and get her."

In a few minutes they were back and I was hauled safely out.

"You naughty girl," Ayah scolded. "Come back to the bedroom at once and let me put some iodine on those scratches." She fetched the bottle from the bathroom cabinet. "That won't look very nice under your pretty party frock."

I grinned at her sheepishly. "I know," I said, "but you're not really cross with me on my birthday, are you? I wish I could have a birthday like this every year."

"I wish you could too," she said, fondly smoothing my hair. "Now put on your dress and go and stand in the porch with Mummy. Then you can say "hello" to your friends as they arrive."

Thinking that her sadness had something to do with my wayward behaviour, I went quietly. It would take a year and a 6,000 mile journey to make me realise the significance of her words and to understand the pain in her eyes.

CHAPTER THREE

LEAVING HOME FOR 'HOME'

I stood with a garland round my neck and a lump in my throat, fighting hard to keep back the tears. The scent of jasmine so close to my face on that hot and sticky May evening was almost unbearable. The thought of leaving that front verandah and never seeing the garland-givers again was more than I could bear. Slowly, the tears spilled over and I knelt hurriedly to join my sister Jane on the floor. She was hugging the dog.

"Good-bye. Be good," she ordered.

Lassie, a Labrador, was tangling herself in the mass of flowers, which had hung almost to Jane's knees when placed round her neck. At four-and-a-half she was small. Much too small and much too young to be leaving home for school in England. She was to be company for me. Seven was the usual age for English children to leave India. I was now seven-and-a-half, and it was I who was crying like the baby of the family. Perhaps it was because I'd had three years longer to cement my loyalties. Perhaps I was more aware of what this parting meant.

They had come one by one to bid their farewells, pressing their hands together in a gesture that wished us well: Cookie and Munswami, the waterman; Muthu, the second bearer; Akshaya, the sweeper; the malis; and Kanaan's wife and children. On behalf of them all, Kanaan, our bearer, had garlanded each one of us, my parents included. He was to come to the station to see us safely off.

But there was one person missing. Esther, Ayah's youngest daughter, who was training to be a teacher at the Mission school, had promised that she would come to say good-bye. To me, Esther was like a sister. A dozen years my senior, she always read me stories, and it was she who had taught me my nursery rhymes and her Tamil songs. It was her long coconut oiled hair I had pulled and later plaited when learning to do my own.

I asked Ayah now. "Why hasn't Esther come?"

"I don't know, Missie, She should be here."

"She promised. Please go and look for her," I begged.

"Don't be long, Ayah," my mother called after her. "We'll have to go in a few minutes."

Ayah was to come with us all the way to Bombay and would be coming back from there with my father. He was not yet able to take home leave, and my mother was taking us on the ship alone. She welcomed the chance of going 'home' on leave. She had not seen her own mother for seven years because of the war.

In the huge porch, under which elephants had once unloaded their passengers, Joseph and Fatty, our drivers, stood by the cars. They too would say 'good-bye' at Madras Central Station. Ayah came back shaking her head and I thought, 'I'll never see Esther again'.

"All ready now, Master." Kanaan had stowed the last of the luggage in the second car.

I looked round at the waiting faces and through the open doors to the dear familiar sitting room with its high ceiling and marble floor. The tiger skin, on whose stuffed head we had sat so often, lay as it always had by the telephone table. On impulse I ran in to pat it, as though for luck, and then I followed the others down the steps.

The servants crowded around as my parents. Jane and I climbed into the first car with Fatty. When we children had nicknamed him thus, it had been as a term of endearment not an insult. The name had stuck. Ayah, Kanaan and the luggage would follow behind with Joseph. There was a babble of voices and Kanaan's children ran, shouting and waving, after us with Lassie at their heels. Then we were through the gate and on our way.

I looked along the roadside, hoping to see Esther there. I remembered the time we had come home, giggling together, in a hand-pulled rickshaw. Riding high up there above the two big wheels had been a treat for me. Usually Europeans only took those rickshaws in an emergency. The cycle rickshaws were faster and perhaps less painful for the conscience. To see a man sweating and straining to pull his load in that torrid heat was not a pretty sight, but such laudable thoughts had not troubled a six-year old.

As usual, porters came jostling for custom at the station entrance. In their faded red shirts, they argued as to who'd been first. My father detailed four of them to carry our belongings to the Bombay Express. Our tin trunks, marked 'Not Wanted on Voyage', had been sent on ahead. We turned now to Fatty and Joseph.

"Good-bye, Anne Missie. Don't forget us." Fatty's plump face was missing its usual beam. He turned to Jane and gently pinched her cheek. "Be a good girl, Little Missie."

Joseph who, like Ayah, was a Catholic, patted our heads. "God bless you Missies. I will pray for you. Good-bye Madam. Until November."

"Come on girls," my father was calling. "The train goes at seven-thirty and we want to get settled."

He led the way, trying to keep the porters in sight. Our bedding rolls were balanced on their heads, extra suitcases wedged under each arm. The whole edifice moved at the half-run, slightly bent at the knees in order to maintain its balance. Surely and rapidly, they threaded their way through the teeming mass to be found at any railway station in India. My mother took Jane by the hand. I grasped Ayah's free one. In her other, she carried a sacking shopping bag with the things she would need for our 40-hour train journey.

Kanaan had gone on ahead to find our reserved compartment. On the platform, the crowd pushed and shoved. People were trying with their bundles and trails of children to find not berths, but just places to sit in the 3rd Class compartments with their slatted wooden seats. It would have been inconceivable for a European to travel anything but 1st Class, but I am glad that in those days there were no air-conditioned carriages. It meant that the smells, the sounds and the colours assaulted the senses and made it impossible for any Indian train journey to be boring.

In 1st Class carriages the seating, which was used at night as sleeping berths, was upholstered in leather. There were upper berths which could be let down, making the compartment into a four, six or eight berth one for a large family. Kanaan had found our six-berth one and was already unbuckling the first bedding roll.

"So when the train starts, Missie, you can go straight to sleep," he told me, knowing full well that there was little chance of that happening.

I remembered the time I had shared my berth with Esther on a short overnight journey to the Hills. We'd woken up at every stop to peer out at the animated melee of an Indian station at night. How I would miss her explanations.

All our train journeys had involved overnight travel. For this, bedding rolls could be hired, but those who stayed in India for any length of time possessed their own. Now Kanaan removed the detachable straps from ours. He unrolled the long canvas strip with its pockets at each end; then folded the side flaps away underneath to expose a crisp white sheet laid over a blanket. From one end, he took and plumped up a pillow. From the other, a second sheet was laid ready to pull over the sleeper. This was not to give warmth, but more as protection against marauding mosquitoes.

After the bedding, Kanaan turned his attention to the provisions for our journey.

"Madam, blue ice box with drinks, red with chicken, scotch eggs and sandwiches," he told her. "Shall I leave towels in bedding rolls or put them in bathroom?"

Each compartment was completely self-contained with its own bathroom. There was a shower, a wash basin and, for the loo, a hole in the floor with the flushing mechanism worked by foot.

"I already locked bathroom window, Master, but I

leave other windows for you."

Each had a choice of three shutters, which could be pulled up and locked into place. The glass one made life impossibly hot, though it did keep out the dust. The wooden shutters kept out the daytime glare while letting in some air. We children disliked the latter because they stopped us looking out. Our favourite was the wire meshing which, while keeping out the thieves, let in the air and allowed us not only to view the passing landscape, but also the crowds and bustle of the stations. These were particularly exciting at night, when we were usually awakened by the bright lights and raucous voices of the vendors.

"Tea, cawfee, arranges," they would shout in English, and again the equivalent in whatever language pertained in that particular part of the country. Bhajis, curry, rice, sweetmeats, all were available; to quench thirst, coconut milk, cane juice and water melons.

Right now, Ayah was outside bargaining volubly in Tamil for a dozen oranges. We hopped down onto the platform to join in the fun. Kanaan followed us.

"Train going soon Missies," he told us, "time to say good-bye."

He put an arm round each of our shoulders and squeezed in a half-hug.

"You learn to write nicely at school, Anne Missie, and send us letters."

He pushed me gently up the steps into the carriage. Then he picked Jane up in his arms and stood her on the top step. Tenderly he pinched her cheek, a gesture of affection for this small child whom he had known from a few hours old because she was born in the house we had just left.

"Good-bye, Little Missie." He turned quickly away and shouted for Ayah to hurry up and get in. The massive steam engine had been hissing noisily for several minutes, though there was no guarantee that the Bombay Express would leave on time.

Suddenly, we heard a shout. Running and weaving her way through the crowd came Esther, her hair tumbling from its chignon, her sari falling down her shoulder.

Breathlessly she explained. "Oh Missies, I'm so sorry. I had to take a class at school and I couldn't find anybody to take over from me. I came as soon as I could."

I tried to lean out of the window to hug her. She grasped each of our hands in hers.

"I'll write you letters," she said, "and you must write to me."

Choking back the tears, I nodded. At least I had seen her again.

My mother went to the door with last minute instructions to Kanaan about the house.

"Don't worry Madam, I looking after Master," he told her, and we knew he would.

My father thrust a fistful of notes into Kanaan's hand.

"See you next week," he told him.

I wished so much that I could say the same. There was some loud clanking and hissing, then a piercing whistle as the Bombay Express slid slowly out of Madras Central Station.

REMEMBER ME SOMETIMES

"Will Ayah come on the boat with us?" asked Jane.

"Only to say good-bye," I answered my four-year old sister in a whisper.

Tears welled up in Jane's eyes as she turned to look at the sleeping figure of our Indian nursemaid on the berth opposite.

"I don't want to go away," she said in a tight, choking voice.

"Nor do I," I replied, "but Mummy says all English children have to go to school in England."

I glanced at the upper berths, where our parents slept on oblivious. We sat cross-legged and whispering on a berth below. White sheets wrapped around us like shrouds kept out the chill morning air. As the Bombay Express sped through villages and paddy-fields, we looked out at wakening India.

From mud huts stumbled children rubbing the sleep from their eyes. Women sluiced their faces with water and wound their bright saris. Others were lighting fires to prepare the first meal of the day. Men, already on their way to the fields, had stopped to perform daily routines. On waste ground, backs turned, they squatted in that posture so familiar that we children had long stopped embarrassing people by asking what they were doing. Small boys, sticks in hand, guided their buffalos to muddy pools. Cows, secure in their sacredness, were left to find their own grazing. Scraggy poultry wandered freely too, on the hard-baked ground of the villages. Occasionally a cockerel loudly heralded the start of a new day: a day we all knew would soon surrender its morning cool to the heat of a blazing sun.

In the compartment, our parents were now washing and dressing. Ayah had re-wound her coconut oiled hair into its bun at the nape of her neck. She handed us clean clothes and bent to fasten Jane's shoes. Jane leaned over and hugged her.

'She'll have to learn to do up her own buckles,' I thought, dreading the loss of my dear comforting Ayah.

"Anne Missie, stop dreaming and hurry up," Ayah admonished. "Next station Spencer's man bringing breakfast."

Spencer's was the company that did the catering for 1st Class passengers on the railways. Not for us the hot steaming tea or coffee, already mixed with milk and sugar, and poured from urns into aluminium cups without handles. Not for us the pungent bhajis or samosas passed up through the train windows by grubby hands, which had been waving flies off them for hours. Our breakfast order had been placed the night before and telephoned down the line. It came to us on a salver, borne aloft by a Spencer's waiter confidently pushing his way through the station crowds. His spotless white uniform was cross-banded in the Company's colour of emerald green. On his head, the waving plumes of his matching green pagri (a type of turban) lent a majestic air. He entered our carriage and set down our tea and toast with a flourish. The tea cosy, tea strainer and sugar tongs were all in place. Behind him, a second minion with an even larger tray removed the silver plated covers to reveal scrambled eggs and bacon. Even the marmalade was there.

"Master wanting any ice, sodas, lemonades?" the white clad figure asked.

Our ice-box, carefully packed by Kanaan the night before, needed replenishing and the second minion was despatched for fresh ice.

"We'll order lunch now," my father told him, "but only for Madam and me. The girls can have chicken and sandwiches from the ice-box, and we'll eat at Guntakal."

"Daddy, are you going to get off and leave us all by ourselves?" asked Jane anxiously.

"You'll have Ayah here, darlings" replied my mother, "and the train won't leave without us."

She knew this was our great fear. We children, at seven and four, were considered too young to go to the station restaurant, but on long journeys the adults often left the train to eat. At junctions, where the stops were long, Spencer's usually had dining facilities. We were never happy until we saw our parents back on the train.

At Guntakal, we pestered Ayah with questions. "Have you got the tickets, Ayah? Did Daddy give you any money? What will we do in Bombay if we leave Mummy and Daddy behind?"

"Don't be silly, Missies. Station Master won't blow whistle till all Europeans are back on train," she replied. "Now, you look out of the window and tell me if you see the tiffin man. I want to buy a nice bryani for my lunch."

We scanned the crowds. I let down a shutter and pushed my head out of the window to see what transactions were being carried out down the length of the train. The traders were doing good business.

"Mangos, plantains, arranges," shouted a vendor, walking slowly towards us, his basket of fruit balanced on his turbaned head. I turned to look in the other direction.

"Oh look Ayah, there's the bangle man. Can we buy some bangles? Please, Ayah?"

"Yes, please Ayah, please," Jane pleaded too.

We loved doing business with the bangle man, who was a travelling salesman carrying his wares in a bundle from place to place. He sold bangles of glass in all colours of the rainbow and an assortment of sizes. Today, many are made of plastic, but it is still the glass ones that shimmer and tinkle the most — especially if you buy eight or ten of them to jangle all the way up your arm. You could buy them of all one colour to make a big splash of red or gold or green. You could buy each in a different colour, or choose the shades to grade from palest sky to indigo. The secret was to buy exactly the right size so that the bangles slipped easily over your thumb knuckle, but were still small enough not to fall off when you dangled your hands downwards.

"Look Ayah, he's coming over now," said Jane, who was already beckoning him.

"No Missie, not today," replied Ayah. "If you go on the ship with bangles and the sea is rough — I don't want you falling over and cutting yourself."

"But we'll take them off Ayah. We'll take them off and keep them until we get to England."

"Missie, little girls don't wear bangles like that in England. Anyway, I don't have enough money to buy bangles for you."

I looked at Ayah in consternation. I knew she would have bought us anything we wanted if she'd had the money. Generosity was only one of the qualities for which we loved her.

"I don't think England sounds a very nice place," said Jane.

"You had better tell him to go away," I told her.

"I wish Mummy and Daddy would hurry up and come back," she replied. "Daddy would buy us some bangles. Look, look at the lovely red ones."

The man was already showing her the choicest of his wares; the ones with the gold specks that sparkled when the sun caught them.

"No, we don't want any bangles today," I told him.

"You buy, Miss-sahib — very cheap," he urged. "I show you many lovely bangles."

He was unloading his bundle from his back. In it, he carried cylinders of different sizes on which his bangles sat snugly and safely. He also carried soap and water to help ease the glass over any knuckle that was too big for one size but too small for the next.

"No," I told him firmly. "Go away."

Ayah came to the window and told him in no uncertain terms to stop pestering us, and to send the bryani man over if he saw him. The man seemed to understand her, though they spoke different languages.

Suddenly, the train shuddered.

"Oh, we're going, we're going," cried Jane. "Can you see Mummy and Daddy? Are they coming back?"

The engine was hissing, people were shouting and

pushing their way into already crowded 3rd Class carriages.

"Yes, here they come," I answered.

A wave of relief swept over me as my parents climbed back into the train. The bangles were forgotten as they told us what they had ordered for our supper and handed out the sweets they had brought.

The afternoon passed with Jane and I playing a game of snakes and ladders between watching the landscape. A hot wind blew dust in at the window, but it was preferable to no wind at all. Now we were crossing the Deccan plateau, almost in the middle of the sub-continent, and the colour of the earth had changed to a noticeable red. The people too looked different; not as dark as our own Tamils, and some of the women wore their saris caught up between their legs. In Madras, it was only the coolie women who did this while they were working on a building site.

Towards 6.30 pm, the sun had become a deep red ball on the horizon. My parents took out the whiskey bottle. Wherever he was in India, no self-respecting Englishman — or woman — would go without his burra (large) or chota (small) peg at sundown. According to legend, it kept the stomach bugs at bay and consuming at least two per evening was a necessary habit, which few retired India hands ever manage to break. After 40 years in India, my father certainly didn't, and neither my mother after only 35 years!

At the next stop, we called in the sweeper woman to brush out the compartment with her broom of dried grasses tied in a bunch. Jane remembered the bangle man and looked out in vain for another.

Our second night on the train we dozed through most of the stops. The novelty of our journey had begun to wear off and we were tired with the noise and the heat. Ayah's white sari was looking decidedly limp and grey. Our hair was thick with dust and, if the constant showers we took kept us cool, they did not keep us clean for long.

"Well girls, we're due in Bombay at eleven this morning," my father told us over breakfast.

"If we don't see a bangle man before then, will you buy us some in Bombay, Daddy?" Jane had not forgotten her quest.

"Darling, I don't want you running around with glass bangles on the ship," said my mother. "You could break them and hurt yourself."

"You see Missie, that's what I told you." Ayah was rummaging in her sacking shopping bag. "But Janie, if you want bangles so badly, then come here." She had found what she wanted and was opening a small cardboard box. "I was waiting to give you these when we said good-bye."

She had produced four silver bangles and was handing two to each of us.

"I want you to remember your old Ayah whenever you wear them."

She helped us slip them onto our wrists. They were fashioned in such a way that they would expand as we grew.

I threw my arms around her and knew that she must have saved for months to buy us such a gift. More than seventy years later I still have the bangles, and it is not only when I wear them that I remember my dear Ayah.

PULLING UP THE ROOTS

The noise and bustle of Bombay's Victoria Station engulfed us — two little girls clutching our most treasured belongings. We had ended one journey only to begin another. What lay ahead was uncharted territory and my sister Jane wasn't entering it without her beloved Mungo. Mungo was a small ragged teddy-bear to whom she had turned for consolation all the four years of her life. She hugged him tightly now, as I clutched the little attaché case in which I'd packed my glass animals. They were a collection I had begun two years ago on my fifth birthday and now they were going to England with me. We'd given many of our toys to the servants' children, and most of those we were keeping had been packed into big tin trunks and sent on ahead for the ship's hold. But Mungo and the glass animals and some books had been allowed to travel with us. In fact, without Mungo, I don't think Jane would have left Madras at all. She turned now and grasped Ayah's hand.

"Where's Daddy?" she wanted to know.

"Gone to find the Brindley's man," answered my mother. "He is supposed to meet us here and take our suitcases. Then we need only take our overnight things to the hotel."

We stood, dirty, hot and tired after our train journey, three white faces amidst a sea of brown ones. The other Europeans who had been on the Bombay Express had already departed, their luggage whisked away by porters in their uniform of red shirts. They had besieged the train as it came in, clamouring for our luggage. The four my father had chosen were getting impatient.

"Madam, porter asking if you want taxi," Ayah ventured on their behalf.

"No, Mr. Mackenzie is sending his car," my mother replied. "His driver should have found us by now."

Mr. Mackenzie ran the Bombay branch, as my father ran the Madras branch, of the same insurance company.

'Finding us can't be easy,' I thought as the crowd pushed past carrying bundles, baskets and children on their way to the exit.

"Ah, there he is, and there's Mac too." A tall red-haired man was pushing his way through to us.

"It is good of you to come and meet us, Mac," my mother exclaimed above the babble.

"Yes, I was going to call into the office to see you this afternoon," said my father, who had reappeared with the shipping agent.

"I thought we might all have lunch at your hotel," said Mac. He turned to us. "And you must be Jane and Anne."

"She's Anne and I'm Jane, and this is our Ayah," Jane volunteered. "She can't come to England with us. Same as Daddy."

"Yes, it's a pity they can't spare you to go on leave yet, old man," said Mac to my father, who was due to follow us in two months' time. As an employee of a British insurance company, my father was a 'boxwallah' and not one of the 'heaven sent' or 'heaven born' like those representing the ICS (Indian Civil Service), as his father had. Next in the Raj hierarchy came Indian Army officers, and only then 'boxwallahs' or employees of business companies amongst whose ranks Banking and Insurance companies rated higher than Trading companies, followed by Retail companies and shops. It was not only the Indians who operated a caste system!

Mac now addressed us, "I'll take you two and your ayah in my car and your Mummy and Daddy can take the luggage in the other." We drove through chaotic traffic to the hotel. It was an imposing building. While my father booked us in I gaped, round-eyed with wonder, at the marble columns and the sweeping staircase. Even more fascinating were the people, especially the females. They were dressed in vivid saris with gold embroidery and wide gold borders. Some of the European women wore elaborate hats. I wondered if they were going to a wedding. The men were less ostentatious — at least those who were guests. Some of the staff looked quite splendid, their white uniforms banded with scarlet, their pagris (a type of turban) waving as they scurried to and fro. We were assigned rooms on the third floor, overlooking the sea.

"Look down there," said Jane, awestruck, as we stood on the landing while the room-boy showed my parents their room. Few who have stayed in the old part of Bombay's Taj Mahal Hotel forget their impression of its central well surrounded on each floor by marble corridors and ornate railings; especially if the sun is streaming through the glass roof making intricate patterns of the shadows. Then Ayah shepherded us into our room, while the room-boy set the fan whirring.

We rushed over to the window and tried to peer through the blinds. "Oh look, look, the sea. Ayah, please pull the blind up," I begged.

"That making room hot, Missie." she warned.

"We can put it down afterwards," I told her.

I peered downwards to the road. The sparkling sea lapped against the wall on its far side. From below us came the plaintive sound of a snake-charmer's flute. His cobra, swaying mesmerised in front of him, was certainly attracting the tourists.

An hour later, bathed and dressed in clean clothes, we ate lunch in the hotel dining room. We found the sheer extent of white-clothed, silver-laid tables intimidating and were on our best behaviour. As the adults lingered over coffee, we grew impatient.

"Can we go outside?" I asked.

"Not without Ayah," my mother replied, "and she's gone to find herself some tiffin."

"Alright girls," said my father, "we'll go and get your topis (pith helmets) and then I'll take you for a ride in a gharry. We'll go down to the bazaar and buy some mangos. You won't get those in England I'm afraid."

"What's a gharry?" I wanted to know.

"It's a horse-drawn carriage. In England, only the King and Queen ride in one of those."

My father liked Bombay. As a bachelor he had spent three years in the Company's office there. We went out and found a gharry. The horse was thin and mangey and the grizzled old man who sat up front and drove was too. After some fierce bargaining, he and Dad agreed the fare. From the toothless smile he gave us as we climbed aboard, I guessed our driver had come rather well out of the transaction.

We climbed into the carriage, which had definitely seen better days — probably Queen Victoria's.

"I hope there won't be too many fleas in these seats," said my father. "We don't want you going on board scratching like a couple of monkeys."

We set off at a fast trot, which generated a breeze. It made the afternoon sun bearable but we were glad we had our topis. I doubt that the carriage canopy would have survived being pulled into place.

Our pace slowed as we neared the bazaar as the streets had narrowed and the crowds become more dense, more voluble. Our driver deposited us at the entrance to Crawford Market. Founded in 1871, this Market covers a vast area of more than 72,000 square yards, and is noteworthy for its splendid architecture. We were impressed by the clock tower, which is adorned with intricate Victorian carvings. Apart from fresh fruit and vegetables, its produce includes meat, poultry, cheese, chocolate, and much else.

It was cool inside the brick building. As our eyes became accustomed to the dimmer light, we could see that we had come into the flower section. The fragrance of jasmine hit us as we passed the women making garlands, and the hair decorations, which many Indian girls tuck into their chignons or plaits. Some sat cross-legged and suckled their babies, whilst around them, stacked in great bunches in buckets and tins were splashes of pink and purple zinnias, tall red cannas and yellow sunflowers. Ignoring the cries of "Sahib, Sahib", my father led us on to the fruit and vegetable section.

Here some of the vendors had stalls, but others had laid out their wares on the ground. There were stacks of watermelon, some cut to show their juicy red interiors; plump mangos nestling in baskets of straw; piles of ripe papayas, and plantains, green and red, as well as the humble yellow banana. By now, we had collected a retinue of small boys with baskets, all offering to carry our shopping. We knew enough Hindi to tell them to go away, but if they did understand us they preferred to take no notice. My father chose our mangos by feel and smell; the Alfonse ones we liked the best. He paid without bargaining the price demanded by the wizened old woman. The trail of boys followed us out to the sunlight.

It was at bedtime that Jane discovered the absence of Mungo. We searched both rooms.

"I can't go to sleep without him," she sobbed. "Where has he gone?"

The room-boy was called.

"I not seeing anybody, Sahib," he told my father guardedly, as if the room had been burgled rather than a stuffed toy lost. "But I off duty this afternoon."

"It can't have been a thief," said my mother. "There's nothing else missing. I'm sure we'll find him in the morning, when we pack."

Jane was finally coaxed to bed and was so tired that she soon fell asleep.

To me, sleep didn't come so easily. I lay and listened to the sea breaking against the wall below, trying to remember when I had last seen Mungo. When Ayah came to lay out her mat on the marble floor beside my bed, my thoughts turned to her. It was bad enough that Jane had lost Mungo, but after tonight Ayah too would not be with us. It was the last time ever that she would sleep there beside me, ready for anything that happened in the night. I dreaded the thought of life without Ayah. She had been like a rock; always there when I needed her, with the end of her white sari to wipe away my tears.

I asked, "Come and lie on the bed with me Ayah?"

"No Missie, Madam wouldn't like it."

"Alright then, I'm coming to sleep on the floor." I climbed down with my pillow.

I knew I could sleep on the floor, but not like Ayah, with only a wad of clothes folded up under her head. I lay down and felt the comfort of her body next to mine. Then I turned on my side towards her and fell asleep. I don't know how much later I found her laying me back in my bed. Sleepily, I put my arms round her neck and gave her a hug. "I love you Ayah," I told her, and closed my eyes once more.

Next morning was one big rush, punctuated by anguished cries from Jane. "Oh Mungo, please come back! Where are you Mungo? I don't want to go without you." Mungo stayed missing.

"We'll ask the hotel people to post him on if they find him," my mother reassured her.

"And this afternoon I'll go back to the market and to the station to see if he's there," promised my father. "We'll look in Mac's car too."

After breakfast, the office car arrived to take us to the docks. As we left the hotel someone was calling "Sahib,

Sahib". It was our gharry man calling from across the road.

"A gharry is the last thing we want this morning," muttered my father, distractedly waving at the old man.

We all squeezed into the car. I sat next to Ayah, while Jane climbed onto her lap.

"Have you found a little teddy-bear?" she demanded of the driver.

"No Missie Baba, not in this car or the other one."

At the docks, the Brindley's man took us through port formalities. He led us onto the quayside. I had never seen a liner so close by before. Its white hull dotted with dark portholes loomed above us. Solemnly, we followed the Brindley's man up the gangway. My father brought up the rear, after the porters with our suitcases on their heads.

'Quite exciting,' I thought. Jane was holding tightly to Ayah's hand as we threaded our way through noisy crowds, and then through interminable corridors, to a tiny dark room with four berths. 'So this is what they called a cabin'. I followed a single shaft of light and found we had a porthole at the end of a little passage.

"What if the water comes in?" I asked.

"No, it's tightly closed — look." My father reassuringly tugged at a handle.

Ayah, cosseting us to the end, was already hanging our clothes into a cupboard.

"I don't want to go," said Jane suddenly. "I don't want to leave Daddy. I don't want to leave Ayah, and I don't want to leave Mungo. He'll be frightened now, all alone somewhere." She started to cry.

I wanted to cry too. I had seen that Ayah's brown face

was already streaked with tears.

"Daddy will be coming to England soon, darling," my mother was trying to tell Jane.

"But Ayah won't," she sobbed.

Suddenly the loudspeaker crackled into life.

"All visitors ashore please. The ship is about to sail. All visitors ashore."

We hugged Daddy. We hugged Ayah. My tears were flowing freely now. We followed them up on deck and stood by the rail as they joined the stream of people descending the gangway. There seemed to be a commotion at the bottom. Someone was wanting to come up. My father had reached the bottom now. Suddenly he turned and shouted. He was waving his arm and there was something in his hand.

"It's Mungo, it's Mungo!" Jane cried joyfully.

My father bounded up the gangway, pushing his way past the remaining people.

"The gharry man brought him," he said. "He was in the gharry, Janie."

She grabbed her bear and kissed him. Then my father kissed us all again.

"You'll give him a big bakshees (tip), won't you Daddy?"

"Of course I will, Janie." I thought he was going to cry too.

He turned and went quickly down the gangway as they prepared to pull it up.

They stood there in a row. My father, tall and fair, next to our dumpy little Ayah in her white sari, and finally, the toothless old gharry man. They made an incongruous picture; my picture of the India I loved. The ship began to shudder and draw slowly away from the quayside. There was a loud boom from the siren as the tugs guided the great white liner out to sea.

"Come on," said my mother. "Let's go to the back of the ship. We'll get a better view from there."

Behind us our shimmering wake slapped against Apollo Bunder, on which stood the Gateway of India. Story has it that there is no more welcome sight to an Englishman than that monument seen from the stern of a liner bound for Britain. Legions of colonials are supposed to have tossed their topis into the sea as a last gesture of their escape.

I had no wish to escape, and I did not realise then that that land would never set me totally free. I had been born into my own favourite place on the planet, far from where my passport and heritage said I belonged. Now, with regret that was nevertheless tinged with a certain excitement, I was to re-establish my roots. Standing there, I had no idea how difficult that would be.

CHAPTER FOUR

ENGLAND: THE UNKNOWN

I awoke and rushed to the porthole. Today was the day we were going to arrive in England, and I wanted to know whether we had reached there yet. Yes, England was to be seen, and it struck me as a very green place. The ship on which we had travelled thousands of miles from Bombay had tied up at Plymouth Docks and Plymouth Sound was sparkling in the May sunshine. I turned to my mother. "Can we get off now?"

"As soon as we've had breakfast," she replied. "We must look out for Aunt Mary. She is coming from London to meet us."

Aunt Mary was my mother's younger sister, and I didn't know what she looked like because the last time I had seen her was when I was a bridesmaid at her wedding in Madras at the age of two. Jane had never met her, but we had heard a lot about her and knew that she had a son, Brian, the same age as Jane. I wondered if he too would be coming to meet us.

Suddenly there was a knock on the door, it burst open and a pretty lady threw her arms around my mother and hugged her. Then she hugged Jane and me. Somehow, Aunt Mary had managed to talk herself on board.

"I told them you had two little girls and would need help with your luggage," she said. We all went for breakfast. Exceptionally, we were allowed to eat with the adults.

After we had packed up and said good-bye to our long-suffering cabin steward, we made our way carefully down the gangway.

"Now we have to look for the 'R' section," said my mother, "because the rest of our luggage will have been unloaded there."

All baggage travelling on the ship had to carry a label with the first letter of one's surname printed large upon it. In the shed on the dockside, the Customs men worked their way through the alphabet, interviewing each family and sometimes examining their luggage before declaring them free to leave. It was no good being impatient if one's name started with a W or a Y.

Eventually, we were able to find a porter to take our luggage to the train to London. The heavier cases and trunks would be transported by arrangement with a carrier and sent direct to our final destination, which was Bedford. In London we had to change stations and the journey to St. Pancras was a revelation to Jane and me. We had never seen taxis in which the seats folded down and where suitcases could be stacked next to the driver. We were impressed by the huge red buses we passed.

When we boarded the train to Bedford, I noticed that we were travelling 3rd Class, but to my surprise, the seats were upholstered and the train had corridors. In India, 3rd Class carriages had wooden bench seats, which were always packed with people and their bundles; we never travelled 3rd Class.

It didn't bother me at all to go down the social escalator. It might have bothered my mother; it definitely bothered other ex-pats who grew rather used to their exalted status in India and struggled with being merely normal on their trips home. But my first experience of rubbing shoulders with the average Englishman in a 3rd Class carriage was just fine. In fact, of all the gifts that India has shared with me over the years, one has been a feeling of comfort with whomever and wherever I happen to be.

In Bedford, a taxi took us to a place my mother kept calling 'home'. Anything less like my home I couldn't imagine. Everything was so strange and different, and the middle-aged lady we met there was a stranger. She was our maternal grandmother, and she lived in a two-storey detached house with quite a big garden. She rushed out to welcome us and clasped us in turn to her ample bosom. She had seen me as a baby the last time my mother had been able to get home from India, just before the war began. Of Jane she had seen only photographs. Then we met cousin Brian, a little boy of four with red hair, who seemed pleased to see us, or at least his mother, because she worked in London and Grandma, who was a widow, looked after him during the week.

Also there to meet us was a grandparent from my father's side. Grandpa Pop, as we came to call him, had lodged with Grandma since the death of his wife. Working for the I.C.S. (Indian Civil Service), he too had spent many years living in India, and must have known from experience with his own boys, that we would be finding everything strange and a little bewildering.

The adults were all chattering excitedly, and Brian was told to show us where we would sleep. We were to have a

Grandma, with whom we spent five years in Bedford

room upstairs, leading off our parents' room. One of the things we found difficult at first was going to sleep while it was still light. We were not used to long summer evenings and, even with the curtains drawn, tended to stay awake and then part them to peer out at the people passing by in the street. The front garden of the house was narrow and had, right outside our window, a pear tree which overhung the hedge. When the pears began to ripen, passing youths tried to pull down the boughs to pick the fruit. They took little notice of our loud taps on the window pane.

Jane and I had to get used to people taking less notice of us. Whereas in India we had been the apples of our servants' eyes, and particularly the centre of our Ayah's attention, here in England the grown-ups seemed to have so many things to do that we felt we were ignored. So we very much appreciated Grandpa Pop's attempts to introduce us to some English pleasures. It was he who taught us how to make daisy chains, pointing out the buttercups and daisies that grew on the grass verge outside the house. Sometimes he took us with him when he went fishing and showed us how to catch tadpoles in a net.

The River Great Ouse ran past the end of our road and, in a field next to it, an artificial lake had been formed. On it, people could hire rowing boats and pedal boats. I was thrilled at being allowed to take out a pedal boat and was told to listen carefully for my allotted number calling me in at the end of fifteen minutes.

After two or three months, my parents engaged a nanny for us. They were due to return to India after six months' leave and decided it was too much to ask my grandmother to look after us without help; particularly as she suffered from sciatica and had trouble walking. Nanny Hoofe arrived and took us for walks in the park, where we enjoyed the children's playground, and on bus trips to the centre of town. We never travelled on buses in India, though we were quite used to rickshaws.

The photograph my parents took back to India when leaving us in England. From right: my mother, Jane and myself

An important occasion was when my mother took me to buy my school uniform. I was due to start at Bedford High School for Girls in September and was intrigued by the amount of clothing I had to have. Apart from skirts, blouses and jumpers, there was a blazer with the school crest on the pocket; a tie in house colours, determined by the area in which you lived; a felt hat banded in the same blue and silver for my house, St. John's, and finally the voluminous navy bloomers, quite alien to me, which I would wear for gym if not at all other times. The items for which I was most grateful were the navy woollen gloves because, when winter came, my hands seemed to freeze and I sometimes arrived at school feeling sick and faint. On several occasions, I missed the morning's first lesson because the school nurse took me into the Sick Room to recover.

I was just eight when I started in the First Form at Bedford High School. It was a huge building and quite overwhelming for somebody who had only been at school with a handful of pupils tutored by one of her playmate's mothers. There were strange rituals like changing your shoes for indoor ones whenever you came in from the playground; no talking in the cold, draughty corridors through which hundreds of us marched each day to the vast assembly hall for morning prayers; and homework to be done. In my first week, I was asked to write a composition and draw a picture to illustrate it. I was in tears and didn't know where to start. Finally, I wrote out something suggested by my mother and persuaded her to draw a picture. Obviously, the latter gave me away, and I was scolded for getting a grown-up to help me, and never tried that again.

The part I did enjoy was morning break. The play-ground was spacious with plenty of room for hop-scotch and games of tag. Best of all, we were each given half-a-pint of milk to drink, and if you paid for it, a sticky raisin bun. We went home for lunch and often in the afternoon had games. The playing fields and changing rooms were on a grand scale, and in my first year I learned to play netball and rounders, later graduating to hockey, tennis and cricket.

Gymnastics was a lesson I knew nothing about. The gym was enormous with wall-bars, climbing ropes and something called a horse which, in later years, I was expected to vault. I found the prospect terrifying. In fact, the whole experience of England was turning out to be far from the pleasant adventure I had imagined. For my little sister, Jane, who was enrolled at a primary school together with Brian, it must have seemed even more daunting.

Worse was to come. As summer turned to autumn, the realisation began to dawn that soon our parents would no longer be with us. Our grandparents were kind and we were not being sent away to boarding school, but my father's leave was coming to an end and he would not be able to visit England again for two-and-a-half years. My mother would be coming back for three months the following summer, but to an eight-year old and a five-year old, a year seemed an impossibly long time. I was told the months would soon pass, but I dreaded the parting.

Then, one November morning, after a lot of packing and hustle and bustle, the taxi came to take my parents away. I could not stem my tears and Jane clung pathetically to my mother's hand. The luggage was loaded, we said our tearful good-byes, and the car drove off down the road. Grandma and Grandpa Pop put their arms around us and hugged us, but nothing could take away the feeling of sheer desolation that engulfed me as the taxi turned the corner and vanished from sight.

ACCEPTING ENGLAND

With our parents having returned to India, Jane and I were miserable, but after awhile, the daily routine of school, where we were making new friends, began to occupy our minds. Children are resilient. And we were constantly distracted by learning how to cope with our new lives. It was not only in lessons that we were learning new things. When we went shopping with Grandma, we saw how she had to produce ration books from which coupons were cut for most of the things we ate. She explained that during the war, which had just ended, food had been and still was scarce, and so people were limited in the amount they could buy. To our dismay, this also applied to chocolate and sweets and, despite all the exciting new varieties available in England, we could not indulge as we'd have liked. There was the compensation that we could buy ice cream and eat it on the streets — something we would never have done in India, where all our ice cream was made at home or at the Clubs of which my parents were members. Grandma loved ice cream too, and often sent us round to the dairy a few streets away to buy ourselves some and bring back a tub for her.

Another pleasure was the Children's Library, to which my grandfather introduced me. I began with stories about a bear called Mary Plain and, during my five years at school in England, read my way through all the Enid Blyton, graduating to series on 'Anne of Green Gables', 'Sue Barton – Special Nurse', and even 'Biggles', followed by 'Swallows and Amazons'. Looking back, I think it was a way of escaping from the fact that I was no longer with my parents and missed them dreadfully.

The thought of Christmas without them was dismal. However, Brian's mother, Aunt Mary, had a treat in store for us. We were to go to London and spend it with her at her flat. Grandma came for three or four days, and Grandpa Pop went to spend Christmas with his 'lady friend', as Grandma called her. But Brian, Jane and I, together with Nanny Hoofe, spent almost the entire school holiday in the capital. Aunt Mary lived in Bayswater and we often went to Whiteley's, which made a huge impression as we were not used to big department stores. We ran up and down the spectacular sweeping staircase, and hid from Nanny, who was inclined to panic when she lost sight of her three charges in, to her, the daunting metropolis of London. She took us to Kensington Gardens, where we gazed at the Peter Pan statue and frolicked in the children's playground. Sometimes we met Aunt Mary at the Wimpole Street consulting rooms of the consultant gynaecologist for whom she worked, and were awed into silence by the plush surroundings. Even more impressive was the theatre to which we were taken to see the pantomime 'Cinderella'.

I had never seen a live stage performance before and was captivated both by the actors and the sumptuous red and gold interior of the venue.

On Christmas Eve, I had difficulty getting to sleep. I could hear not only the traffic of a big city, but also the shouting and hilarity of celebrating drunks passing on Westbourne Grove. From the window, I could see the big red London buses on which I had recently ridden for the first time. I had enjoyed climbing their stairs and watching the crowds from the front seat. Now I was looking out for snow. I had never seen snow and could not imagine what people meant when they talked about 'a white Christmas'.

There was no snow when I awoke on Christmas morning, but there were stockings and presents to open. Later, we went with Aunt Mary to St. Mary's Hospital in Paddington. Because of her connection with the consultant gynaecologist, she was doing a tour of the maternity wards and she took us to see the Mummers, who went from ward to ward performing little sketches. The actors were doctors and nurses, who traditionally dressed up to amuse the patients. We then went home to a lunch of turkey and Christmas pudding, and in the afternoon roasted chestnuts in the fire. Then my grandmother produced her brass Put and Take gambling top which had six sides, each with an instruction: Put One, Put Two, Put All (i.e. double the pot), Take One, Take Two, Take All. We each pooled the same number of matchsticks, and then took turns to spin the top on a big brass tray, which was one of Aunt Mary's wedding presents from India. Depending on which side of the top fell uppermost, we put in and removed matchsticks until one of us spun Take All, when the matchsticks were replaced with pennies by Grandma. According to her, the game was invented in the trenches during the First World War by a soldier, who shaped a brass bullet into a spinning top with six sides, and the stakes he and his mates played for were cigarettes.

Going back to school in January was disagreeable, particularly as I felt the cold so keenly, and I pined for the warmth and sunshine of India. I also pined for my parents and was delighted when my mother came back earlier than expected. She arrived in April because she was expecting a baby in June. Jane and I were excited at the idea of a baby brother or sister, but above all, we had our mother back.

She took me to buy my summer school uniform: blue and white gingham frocks and a straw hat, again banded in blue and silver. I also needed a regulation navy swimming costume because swimming lessons were part of the school curriculum. At last, I thought, there would be something I was good at. The school did not have its own pool but we were allowed use of the one at Bedford School, the boys' equivalent of the High School. Also, there was a public swimming pool at the end of our road and, as I loved swimming, I elected to be taken there as often as possible.

We were also taken to the country to learn to ride. My grandmother knew a farmer who had ponies near the village of Thurleigh, and he was chosen to give us riding lessons. I suspect he was also chosen because he was prepared to supply us with eggs to eke out the meagre rations. Jane, Brian and I were kitted out with jodhpurs and hard hats, and we drove to Thurleigh once a week in

Grandma's old Singer. She always had difficulty backing it out of the garage, so I think was glad when my mother arrived and took over the driving. It was something she could help with because, having gone out East to marry my father at the age of twenty, she had always employed a cook and her culinary skills were limited.

The story of how our parents met always amused us children. On his first home leave in Bedford, my father was walking past a photographer's and saw a portrait of a girl in the display window. He told us he thought she was beautiful and said to himself, "That's the girl I'd like to marry." Some weeks later he walked into the Bedford branch of the insurance company for which he worked — and there she was, sitting behind a typewriter. At the end of his leave, he was posted to Malaysia, and a little more than a year later, he wrote and proposed. My mother travelled out by sea, chaperoned by acquaintances, with her wedding gown in her suitcase. They were married two days after her arrival in Singapore.

So Grandma did all the cooking for us and, despite the rationing, managed to feed us well. In the summer we had plenty of fruit from the garden, where there were apple, pear and plum trees, but the one thing we missed was bananas. They only appeared in the greengrocer's sporadically, and then long queues formed and they were soon snapped up.

As the weeks went by, my mother grew bigger and bigger, and we kept asking her when the baby would arrive. One night in late May we awoke to a commotion. Outside was an ambulance with lights blazing, and we watched from the window as my mother was carried to it on a stretcher. We were told that the baby would soon be here, but a few days later my mother returned without a baby. It had been a false alarm, and she then went to London to stay with Aunt Mary so that she could give birth at Queen Charlotte's Hospital, which was the original plan. For the next few nights I had nightmares in which my mother had died so we would never see her again. But all was well, and our baby sister, Susan, was born in June. So it was with relief and delight that we welcomed them back to Bedford a week later. We did not have them with us for long. A couple of months later, after another sad parting, they returned to India to join my father.

Jane and Brian take Sue for a walk in the park

LEAVING ENGLAND

During the five years we were in England, my parents together with our baby sister, Sue, came back from India for just one Christmas. It was the winter of 1947/1948, and my grandmother had to go into hospital in London to have a skin graft on her leg, where an ulcer had become a large hole. It meant that my mother had to cook Christmas lunch, a task for which she lacked both confidence and competence. She'd never cooked. When she'd been home, Grandma did. Then she left for the East and Cookie did. Jane and I didn't care; we were just delighted to have our parents with us.

It was a magical Christmas morning with snow outside and our parents' warm bed to clamber into inside. I remember that in our stockings were stuffed scarlet pixie hoods, which we wore later that morning when we went out to make a snowman and pelt each other with snowballs. My father had not had a Christmas in England for twenty years because he preferred to come on leave in the summer. We, of course, would have preferred our parents to be with us all the time, but it was repeatedly explained that our separations were necessary because it had always been considered unhealthy for English children to stay in the heat of India beyond the age of seven. Fortunately for us, this viewpoint was slowly changing.

For the time being, we continued to live with Grandma. Although she still had trouble walking after her operation, she showed us how to plant seeds in the little patches of garden that Jane, Brian and I were allotted. We grew a profusion of wallflowers and watered them diligently. We climbed the garden's trees and helped pick the apples and plums when they ripened. Our grandfather taught us to ride bicycles and, as I grew older, I was allowed to ride to school instead of going there by bus.

My father with his youngest daughter, my little sister Sue

One year, the River Great Ouse flooded and water began to slowly creep towards us from the end of the road. We hoped it would not reach us, but we did move quite a number of things upstairs. This was just as well, because the water did come into the house and Grandma had to wade to reach the telephone whenever it rang, while we sat on the stairs and wondered how we would get anything to eat. When the water subsided, we found that our dustbins were missing, and my grandparents had to go down the street searching for them. This must have amused me because I wrote an essay about it entitled 'The Flood'. It was my first published work and appeared in *The Aquila*, the school magazine.

When I was ten, I woke one night with an agonising pain in my stomach. The next morning the doctor was called and diagnosed acute appendicitis. I was hurried to hospital in Bedford and operated on. It was yet another occasion when I longed for my mother. Instead, I had for comfort a small stuffed toy bear called Mary Plain, who featured in a series of books for children, and who was made and given to me by a friend of my mother's. In hospital the following two weeks, I read a lot and tried not to laugh when Jane and Brian came to visit me. They were only trying to cheer me up and couldn't know how much it hurt when I laughed or they plonked themselves down on my bed. When I went back to school, I had to sit out the gym lessons and laughed again watching my classmates attempting to vault the horse.

Sometimes, in the summer holidays, we went to stay with my mother's brother, George and his family in

Children of the Raj: All the cousins in the toy train at Littlehampton

Littlehampton. My cousins were also children of the Raj. Of the six of them, four were born in various places near the North West Frontier while their father served with the 1/10th Baluch Regiment of the Indian Army. He, Auntie Di, and the children returned to England after Independence, in the run-up to which, Uncle George was seconded as an advisor to Lord Mountbatten in New Delhi. After working at the Ministry of Defence and for Save the Children, ill health and London's pollution forced him to retire to the cleaner air of the seaside, where he set up a business growing orchids and mushrooms. Of his six children, Marietta was just a year younger than me, and Melanie, his second, was Jane's age. Then came Theresa, Tania, and finally a boy, Tom, before the baby Charlotte, who was Sue's contemporary. So we made quite a gang to play in the garden, go to the beach and ride in the toy train on the sea front. From the jingle-playing van parked there, we ate ice creams and iced lollies, and generally enjoyed a way of life we had not known in India. Poor Auntie Di had a horde to feed, which she managed admirably without the servants she'd become accustomed to in her earlier life.

When I wrote letters to my parents, they often included a request to be taken back to India. For years, these fell on deaf ears, but when my mother came to England in the summer of 1949, she appeared to have had a change of heart. Apparently my parents had been investigating the possibility of sending us to school in India. In the hill station of Ootacamund, where the climate would be healthier for us than that of Madras, they had found a boarding school, St. Hilda's, run by Anglican missionaries, and had decided that they would prefer to have us a few hundred, rather than several thousand, miles away from them. We would have two months' holiday with them in Madras at Christmas, when the temperature was only about 80*F., and another month in the middle of the year when the monsoon rains fell. In April and May, when the weather was very hot in the Plains, and again in September, my mother would come to Ootacamund and take us out of school for the weekends. It was not just my repeated pleas that had made them reconsider, more that they realised that my sister Jane was beginning to regard Grandma as her mother; something my mother was not at all happy about. Though she loved her life in India, she hated being parted from her daughters.

Of course, I was overjoyed at the new plan. When

autumn came, we packed up all our belongings, and waved good-bye to what had been an educative but not relished interlude in our lives.

DESTINATION INDIA

It was with joy in our hearts that, in November 1949, we caught the boat train to Tilbury. Jane, our little sister Sue and I, accompanied by my mother, were to embark in the S.S. Canton, bound for Bombay. When we arrived at the dockside, the ship looked enormous, and we struggled up the gangway to find the Purser's office and check our cabin number. We had a four-berth cabin with a porthole that was difficult to look out of because it was high up, but which gave us some light. Jane and I were allocated the top berths, much to our delight, and immediately tried out the little ladder to get up there.

There was a knock on the door and a young man in a smart white jacket introduced himself as Ritchie, our cabin steward. Little did he know what pests we would be, demanding fruit and lemonade and baths, running up and down the corridors and generally making a nuisance of ourselves. Cabin stewards brought early morning tea; also any food people could keep down if they were seasick. 'Home' going passengers, suddenly depending on their own resources after being cosseted by bearers, ayahs and amahs for two or three years, found them a tower of strength. Ritchie was a great help to my mother, who felt she could safely leave us in the cabin for the evening, knowing that he would keep an eye on us.

There were two sittings for every meal for the adults, and we children, who were considered such up to the age of twelve, had to eat earlier. This meant breakfast at 7:30 am was a bit of a scramble. My mother came with us to oversee Sue, but had her own breakfast at the second sitting at 9:30. Because the children's breakfast never included bacon, we begged that she bring us back bacon butties. At 11 o'clock, stewards toured the decks serving beef tea and, once the weather got warmer, cool drinks and ice cream. This was also the time when we put in our guesses for the ship's run. The person who estimated correctly or was closest to the number of knots the ship had travelled the previous day won a cash prize. The result was announced at midday and we always hoped for but never did win a prize.

Three-year-old Sue was often kept occupied in the ship's nursery, but Jane and I could roam the decks to find our own amusement. We played table tennis and were sometimes asked by friends of my mother to join them at deck tennis or deck quoits. This was a bonus because the courts were always commandeered by adults during the mornings. After lunch, when most of them had retired for a snooze, we were able to play each other on empty courts. They filled up again around 4 pm when many people emerged for tea.

One of the 'uncles' who befriended us was a young man, Roger, who was popular with all the children. According to my mother, he was very shy but he certainly didn't appear so with us. He often wanted to go with us to fetch Sue from the nursery. Once there, he spent ages talking to the purserettes who ran the nursery. After several days, it dawned on me that he always spent longer talking to one particularly pretty girl, Julie, who looked after the children. I sensed a romance and started checking out when she would be there before telling him we were going to fetch Sue.

I don't know whether Roger had hoped and failed to find a wife in England, but he was a tea planter who worked on a tea garden in Assam and probably led a lonely life. Many planters, after their first tour of duty, sought wives when they came on leave to England, and I suspect that Roger was no exception. As the voyage progressed we noticed that he and Julie were often to be seen leaning over the ship's railings, deep in conversation.

"I wonder if he has kissed her yet," I mused to Jane, but we were not allowed up on deck late in the evenings, and never knew how the adults enjoyed themselves at the dances and other activities held each night.

One of the activities arranged for children was the fancy dress tea party, at which prizes were given. Excitement ran high and the ship's shop was swamped by mothers buying up packets of coloured crepe paper and glue. This they cut up and fashioned into grass skirts and exotic flowers for Hula girls, and wings for fairies and angels. Amongst the boys, pirates and cowboys abounded. I went as a gypsy with a borrowed tambourine; Jane as Little Red Riding Hood with my mother's circular red skirt masquerading as a cape, and Sue had a halo and angel wings. First prize was won by a child disguised as a Royal Mail letterbox. His mother must have purloined some cardboard, either from the shop or through her cabin steward, and had covered it in red crepe paper, adding all the appropriate embellishments. Being encased in a cardboard tube could not have been much fun, and he did not wear his outfit for long.

An entertainment that we children particularly enjoyed was the Gully-Gully man. He wore a red fez, baggy trousers and a waistcoat, and was full of patter. He boarded the ship at one end of the Suez Canal and left at the other. Between Port Said and Suez he enthralled us with a succession of tricks, most of which consisted of producing tiny yellow fluffy chicks — real live ones — from various parts of our anatomy.

"Gully, gully, gully," he gabbled, and out popped another day-old chick from a child's nose or ear. We wanted to keep them, but that would have depleted his stock which, at the rate he produced them, struck us as very large. A mystery was where on his person he kept them

We were sorry to see the Gully-Gully man go and to leave the Canal behind us. It had been exciting to see the banks so close as we glided between them, and the sand stretching away into the distance. At the mid-way point we came to the Pool, where liners travelling in the opposite direction had dropped anchor, waiting for their turn to proceed. We were thrilled to see these great ships so near, and leaned over the railings with Julie, Roger, and other passengers, waving and cheering.

Although not allowed up on deck late in the evening, Jane and I were able to wander there while my mother changed for dinner. It was a time when the stewards set out nuts and crisps for passengers to enjoy with their pre-dinner drinks. We helped ourselves liberally, and enjoyed watching the fashion parade as people emerged in long dresses and dinner jackets after their baths. Baths had to be taken in salt water. Tin tubs were placed on wooden slats and over this was a shower. When you wanted a bath, you informed your cabin steward and he called you when a bathroom was free. The only nights that the adults did not wear evening dress were when leaving port or before entering a port the next day.

As we travelled farther east, the men sweltered in their dinner jackets under the dining room fans for there was no air-conditioning. Some of them had white shark-skin dinner jackets, which may have been somewhat cooler, and the ladies were far more comfortable in their strapless evening gowns. The officers changed from dark to white mess kit, and Jane and I fell in love with all of them! They each had their own table for dinner and passengers sat with the same companions for every meal. To be invited to sit at the Captain's table was, apparently, the epitome of success, but not one attained by my mother. Jane and I regretted that we could not watch the after-dinner entertainment, particularly the dancing, but were given a detailed account of the fancy dress dance, and the many ingenious costumes contrived from the limited resources available on board. My mother went as a Hawaian Hula girl. She wore her two-piece swimsuit and a grass skirt painstakingly cut from yards of green crepe paper. Around her neck she wore a garland of paper flowers, which we had helped to make. She told us there were several Hula girls there that evening and none of them won a prize.

The voyage to Bombay took a fortnight, and we began to look forward to seeing our father, who would meet us there for the two-day train journey to Madras. Roger had an even longer journey, as he explained to us on the last evening. He would be travelling for three days, first in express steam trains and then on the Toy Train, which zigzagged its way up to Darjeeling. He was full of smiles and I asked him, "Aren't you sad to be saying good-bye to Julie?"

"Of course," he answered, "but you know what? She has said YES, she will marry me."

CHAPTER FIVE

RETURN TO GRAEMES GARDENS

Graemes Gardens, our home in Madras

As a child of the Raj, the smell of India always transports me back to my happiest childhood days. Now, as we turned into the gates of Graemes Gardens, our bungalow in Madras, a wave of elation swept over me. At the age of twelve I had spent five years at school in post-war England, away from the scorching sunshine, the brilliant colours and exotic smells of the place I called home, though my parents did not; five years away from my beloved Ayah and much of that time away from my parents, which was the worst deprivation of all. I was exultant to be back.

The drive, bordered by oleander trees, led us to the elephant porch in front of the whitewashed house, of which we occupied the ground floor. At the top of the steps, on the front verandah, stood Ayah, Cookie, and Kanaan, our bearer, with garlands of jasmine and marigolds to welcome the family they had served for more than a decade. As were all the servants, they were always kept on to look after the house when my parents went on six months' 'home' leave. Our Labrador barked excitedly and Ayah hugged us three sisters, then held us at arm's length to gauge the changes our absence had brought about.

We ran into the sitting room, where the tiger skin with its stuffed head still lay baring its teeth at us. We ran through the house to see what had changed, but very little had. The oil paintings of race horses still hung on the dining room walls. The silver cups my father had won for his prowess at tennis, squash and badminton stood in rows in the glass-fronted cabinet as they always had. We went through to the back verandah and were greeted with salaams by Munswami, our waterman, and Akshaya, our sweeper. Later we explored the garden and said 'hello' to the mali, who was watering the flower beds in front of the house. Apart from a profusion of flowers, he also raised beautiful ferns in pots, which were placed on the front steps from the huge covered porch to the front verandah. They graced the folly, a strange concrete edifice that rose in circles of steps in the middle of the front garden. There were two lawns shaded by large trees, but the swing we had had in one of them was no longer there. The compound in which the house stood was quite large, and had a chicken run at one side, where my father raised Rhode Island Red hens and a very noisy cockerel. There were guava trees in this part of the garden with scrubby grass below, but no other cultivation. The other side of the compound was considered the servants' territory, where their children, and often we with them, had played.

We did not recognise Kanaan's children, and two more had been produced in our absence. Kanaan's wife came out from their godown to meet us, her hands pressed together in the customary form of greeting. Her long black hair was drawn into a bun at the back of her head, and under her jade green sari I suspected the signs of yet another pregnancy. Kanaan obviously subscribed to the much-held Indian belief that children were an insurance against destitution in old age. How the whole family managed to fit into their cramped living quarters, I do not know, but it seemed they found it preferable to living in the nearby village, which some of our servants did.

Outside her godown, Kanaan's wife had smoothed over a piece of ground with hard baked mud, which she sometimes decorated with patterns drawn with chunam (slaked lime). She was particularly skilled at complex and interweaving patterns drawn with a feather when the slaked lime was wet and allowed to harden. She did it before major holidays to celebrate a religious event. It was, in a way, similar to decorating your house for Christmas.

Further away, there was scrubby grass and one very large tree in which parrots nested. I remembered the time I had asked Kanaan to catch a parrot for us, which we kept in a cage and tried to teach to speak. We made no headway with Polly, and were told that we were being cruel and must set her free.

No exploration of home would have been complete without our climbing the outside staircase to the roof. This was flat but divided into little compartments by low brick walls, making it a great place for hide-and-seek. Now, at dusk, we looked out at the lights coming on over the city, and knew that we must descend soon because darkness fell swiftly.

Later that night there were no heavy blankets on the bed to weigh you down. It was bliss to lie under just a sheet with the whirr of the ceiling fan to lull you to sleep. Unless we were going to a party, there were no socks and shoes to put on, and we ran around in leather chappals (flip-flops), and sometimes in the house, in bare feet. Until we went away to boarding school in the Hills, there would be no more prickly woollen jumpers, and we could wear shorts all day.

In the morning we were delighted to find that Ayah's daughters had come to see us. She had three of them, all educated by Catholic missionaries. Alice, Jeymonie and Esther were now all married, and Esther had brought her little son, David, to meet us. The daughters had often played with us before Jane and I went away to England and had expected never to see us again. It was a joyful reunion.

As we chatted my mother called out, "The monkey man's here. Do you want to watch?"

She knew that this was the animal show we most enjoyed. It was given by two little monkeys, who were made to jump over sticks, to turn somersaults through hoops, and to come up to us with a hat to beg for money. They were very appealing and we wanted to pick them up, but were restrained from touching them on the pretext that they might bite us, but probably because they would almost certainly have given us fleas. Their owner carried them away on his shoulders, but kept a light chain on them in case they decided to run off. He went from house to house giving this performance, and probably earned quite well from it.

Sometimes, wild monkeys came to our compound and swung in the trees, then ate the guavas when they ripened. Many years later, when my father bought a stud farm with a large number of mango trees, monkeys would descend in hordes as the fruit ripened, and became a real nuisance. In the end he had to call in the 'monkey man', an expert at catching the animals, who would take them away and let them loose in some distant habitat. Needless to say, they returned the next mango season.

Mangos and other tropical fruits, and curries and chilli-hot pickles, were all things I had missed whilst away. Right now I could think of nothing I missed about England, except perhaps our grandparents. To be back in India was something for which I'd longed for five whole years, and now at last I was home. It was the best present my parents ever gave me.

SHOPPING OPPORTUNITIES

Being back in India made me extremely happy. We were so pleased to see our servants and their children again, and there was so much to rediscover. When not investigating life round the back of the house, our days were filled with visits to the beach and the swimming pool, tennis practice, and shopping trips with my mother.

When we went shopping, the car was always approached by small boys begging for baksheesh (alms, tips). Some of them were badly maimed and if you took pity on one, who had perhaps dragged himself to you on the stumps of his knees, you were immediately surrounded by a crowd of others, all with outstretched palms. They were a ragged and noisy mob and difficult to shake off until you were able to take refuge in a nearby shop. Callous though this may sound, it was impossible to respond to all the demands. Instead, you learned to avert your gaze and plough on with your chores.

One place where you were not besieged by beggars was the Spencer's car park. Spencer's was the one Madras store. They sold everything, from meat to medication to furniture, and a lot else besides. The tailoring department was where my father had his trousers made, and the cosmetics counter was where my mother bought her toiletries, though she tried to bring most of her make-up out from England. At the front there was a café, where we children begged to be treated to milkshakes and the mothers met for iced coffee. Fatty, our driver, would drop us at the front entrance and, when we were ready to leave, the doorman would shout our car number or name, and Fatty would glide up to collect us. I always marvelled at the way the doormen knew the car numbers of so many customers without any need for prompting. For us, Spencer's was an air-conditioned haven, but Spencer's had other interests besides. They also owned the Connemara Hotel next door, considered to be the best hotel in Madras at that time, and they supplied catering on the Indian railways. At stations, Spencer's waiters, in their white and green uniforms, made an incongruous impression as they wove their way through the motley crowds, bearing aloft their heavily laden silver-plated trays.

My favourite shop was Chellaram's, which sold fabrics. The salesmen were keen to make a sale and nothing was too much trouble. With a flourish, they would roll out yet another bolt of material, extolling its qualities while we dithered amidst a plethora of choice. There were shimmering silks and saris with borders of gold and silver threads; flimsy voiles, crisp taffetas and delicate organdies for ball gowns and party frocks; heavy linens and fine printed cottons, as well as colourful hand-woven khadi cloth. All these were inspiration for amateur fashion designers, as it was not possible to buy ready-made dresses and we had garments made by local tailors. Our own, whom we called MK, was an expert at interpreting a picture or copying clothes brought from England.

We also had shoes made locally, and the shoemaker was usually Chinese. He would come to your home with samples of leather and look at a picture or a shoe that you owned. Then he drew round your foot, took some measurements, and returned some days later with a beautifully made pair of shoes.

Just down the road from Spencer's was the V.T.I. (Victoria Technical Institute), a shop we often visited for Christmas presents. They had an eclectic selection of artisanal items, which made lovely gifts. There were leather goods such as purses, handbags and jewellery boxes; wooden toys; carved ivory and sandalwood pieces; and exquisite embroidery on articles such as table mats, tray cloths and baby clothes. Perhaps most beautiful of all were the organdie tablecloths and napkins with flowers embroidered in shadow-work.

Some of the needlework came from convents, where the nuns took in girls from poor families and, as well as giving them an education, taught them skills such as sewing, which would always stand them in good stead. My mother went often to the Little Flower Convent, where the nuns, some of whom were Belgian, were always pleased to receive orders for smocked dresses and embroidery on lingerie.

Other beautiful embroidery came directly to our front verandah. Itinerant Kashmiri salesmen with bundles on their backs would appear from time to time and try to persuade my mother to buy from a selection of artisanal wares. There were lovely shawls and stoles embellished with vividly coloured silk thread; lengths of hand-woven woollen material with embroidered borders to make into skirts, lacquered papier-mâché boxes, hand-painted with birds and flowers, in which to keep trinkets and sewing items; and sumptuously decorated slippers with turned-up toes. When they had unpacked everything I believe my mother thought that, after all their efforts, they deserved to make a sale. She always bought something, if only a tiny box, but we children benefitted from many a colourful skirt.

Another Kashmiri vendor was the carpet man. He carried a heavy bundle and always arrived at the bungalow early in the morning to catch my father before he went to the office. Although my mother was consulted, he knew that my father, who had some knowledge of oriental rugs, made the final decision on whether to buy one of his beautiful carpets, which came from Isfahan or Bokhara or Kashmir.

My mother's favourite vendor was the haberdashery man, who would untie his bundle and lay out tray after tray containing needles, cotton reels and safety pins; elastic, ribbons and press studs, until he came to the bottom of the pile, where he carried a few bolts of flowered cotton material. He rarely went away without making a sale.

We children loved the bangle man, but he was more likely to go round to the back first because he knew that the servants' wives and children were potential customers. He expected that we would be called to join in the fun of trying on and admiring his brilliantly coloured glass bangles. That we would run inside and persuade my mother to buy us some was virtually a certainty.

The one visitor, who was not supposed to enter our compound at all, was the toddy man. Toddy is a fermented liquor made from the sap of the coconut palm and is extremely potent. People have been known to go blind from drinking too much of it. The toddy man invariably slipped round to the back and my father would have been furious, had he seen him. He transported his brew in two metal vessels slung either side of a long pole that he carried across his shoulders. Kanaan, our bearer, liked the occasional tot of toddy, though we never saw him drunk, and he always begged us, "Missie, don't tell Master," if we ever found him buying a beaker of it. Many years later he returned the favour when, in my late teens, I sometimes came home from a dance at 5 o'clock on a Sunday morning and found him cutting sandwiches for Dad to take on a snipe shoot. "Don't tell Master," I would say and hurry to bed before he woke my father.

Whether any of the other servants partook of the unpleasant smelling liquid, I don't know, but another habit they did indulge in was chewing betel nut. This is the areca nut or seed, which vendors wrap, together with spices and lime paste, in betel leaves and sell in the bazaar. It is said to give a sense of euphoria and wellbeing and colours the saliva red, the spitting of which causes unsightly stains as ubiquitous in India as lumps of chewing gum on pavements in Europe. We never saw our servants chewing on duty, and they made sure there were no stains in places where Master and Madam ventured.

We children, however, were once more welcome throughout the servants' quarters. We spent the two months following our return to India learning a great deal about their lives and otherwise enjoying ourselves, including attending a number of Christmas parties.

CASUARINA CHRISTMAS TREES

Sue – the Queen of Hearts,
at the Gymkhana Club Christmas Party

Out of the car climbed the Queen of Hearts, a Victorian lady, and a bat. My sisters and I had arrived at the fancy dress party given each Christmas time by the Madras Gymkhana Club for the children of its members. Sue, the youngest, came complete with a crown emblazoned with appliqued hearts; Jane carried the beautiful pink parasol my mother had inherited from her grandmother; and from my fingers hung the wings that completed my outfit. I had eschewed the long dresses chosen by the other two and had opted for a short black tunic and a cap with bats' ears.

The Club always arranged for a merry-go-round, a Punch and Judy show, and a Father Christmas to arrive and hand out presents. With no snow a sleigh was out of the question, so he travelled by different means: sometimes on horseback, occasionally in a decorated car; and once even, in a light aeroplane, which landed on the Maidan (open space) next to the Club and caused huge excitement. Though I was too old to believe in Father Christmas, I was nevertheless interested in the spectacle and, of course, in receiving a present. These were chosen by the Committee according to age and gender but were individually wrapped and labelled, so you listened hard for your name to be called out.

All the children sat at long tables to enjoy a delicious spread of sandwiches, cakes, jelly and ice cream. Before Father Christmas was due, we decided to try out the carousel. Sue wanted to ride on a gaudily painted horse with flaring nostrils. "You won't be able to climb on to him in your long skirt," I told her. I persuaded her to get into a carriage purporting to be an engine.

Jane – a Victorian Lady, at the same party

Myself – a Bat, at the same party

"I hope Father Christmas brings me a tricycle to ride on," she said.

I knew this had been her wish in the letter to Santa Claus that she had dictated to my mother. As we had no chimneys up which to send these letters, my mother had always set fire to them in the garden so that we could watch the ashes blow away to Lapland.

Suddenly, people began hurrying across the lawn towards the Maidan. We joined them and watched as a rotund Father Christmas arrived in an open car disguised as a boat complete with sails.

"Follow me, follow me," he called loudly, clanging a bell. We all crowded into the Clubhouse. Around the decorated casuarina tree, which usually stood in for a Christmas tree in India, were piles of presents. The younger children's names were called first and Sue received, to her dismay, a doll and not a tricycle.

"I don't suppose he had room to bring it today," my mother explained to her. "You'll have to wait till Christmas day and see what happens then."

In the week leading up to Christmas we were taken to Moore Market, a huge indoor bazaar, where all the vendors tried to entice us into their tiny shops, and small boys followed us around offering to carry our shopping. We were allowed to choose the decorations for our dining room: brilliantly coloured paper chains that concertinaed down into flat packs and vivid Chinese paper lanterns. Also in these days we witnessed the arrival of the turkey, which was given free range in our garden and fed on plenty of grain to fatten it up. We tried not to think about the fact that it would be our Christmas lunch. The mali found us a large casuarina branch to be decorated as our Christmas tree with the same glass baubles that came out every year. On Christmas morning, we awoke to find bulging stockings, in the striped colours of my father's old rugger team, hanging at the end of our beds. Instead of the traditional orange or apple stuffed in the toe, my parents had hung above our beds a huge branch of bananas for Jane, whose favourite fruit they were, and a large pineapple for me. We ran into their bedroom to unpack our goodies. Then we saw that somebody had strewn flower petals all over the front verandah. It was Kanaan, our bearer's way of marking a special day.

Impatiently, we ate breakfast, waiting for the moment when the doors to the little side room would be flung open to reveal our 'Christmas tree', hung with presents and surrounded by parcels. When I was much younger I had tried to discover what the parcels would contain, and in my mother's large almirah (wardrobe), I had found a beautiful doll. But I had given up the practice because, in subsequent years the drawers revealed only the woollies for hill station visits, kept in calico bags and sprinkled with moth balls and cloves, and long white kid gloves wrapped in tissue paper for receptions at Government House. The beautiful doll had turned out to be a present for Jane.

Now, I was too old for dolls and my Christmas request was for a special bag in which to carry my swimming things, but I was intrigued to know whether Sue would get her wish. She ran in to the room and straight to a mysterious shape in the corner covered by a white sheet. Pulling it off, she squealed with delight, for there indeed was a splendid red tricycle.

"He brought it, he brought it!" she exclaimed, climbing on to it.

"You can't ride it in here," said my mother. "This afternoon you can take it into the garden — the sun is too hot right now."

She began sorting the brightly wrapped parcels until we each had a pile to open. There were presents from friends and presents from various 'aunts' and 'uncles' and yes, from my parents, the beautiful bag I had seen in the shop and wanted so much. A strangely shaped parcel produced a tennis-racquet for Jane. Soon, the sitting room was awash with paper.

At one o'clock, we sat down to lunch and, apart from the fact that it was served by Kanaan and not cooked by my mother, you would not have known that we weren't in England. There were crackers on the table and we wore our paper hats. The turkey was brought in accompanied by roast potatoes and Brussels sprouts and was carved by my father. The brandy around the Christmas pudding was set alight, and Jane found in her portion the silver sixpence which my mother had brought especially from England and instructed Cookie to put into it.

After lunch, it was still too hot to go into the garden, so we were told to rest. Sue found this impossible as she was longing to ride her tricycle. Eventually, at 4 o'clock, we all went outside and watched as she climbed on to her bike. Up and down the drive she rode, pedalling furiously. When she finally came to a stop beside me, she said:

"Isn't it lovely? Father Christmas must have got my letter."

"Yes" I answered, "and I suppose he must have known last week that you wouldn't be able to ride a tricycle in a long dress."

AND THE BRIDESMAIDS WORE PINK

"You're lucky," said Jane wistfully. "I wish I could have a long pink dress like that." Laughing at my nine-year old sister, I twirled, sending the wide silk skirt swishing from its satin waist ribbon.

"Keep still Missie, or pins falling out," warned the derzi (tailor), who had been crawling round me transferring pins from his mouth to a level hemline.

"You had better take it straight off," ordered my mother. "We don't want any accidents before tomorrow." Then turning to Jane, "Never mind darling, you've still got plenty of time to be a bridesmaid. I'm sure Myra would have asked you too, but she only wanted two bridesmaids and Anne and Jennifer Settle are the same height."

Myra had arrived in Madras only a week before. She was staying with my mother's best friend, who was making the wedding arrangements for Myra and Bob, one of the assistants in her husband's office. The young man had recently been on home leave and had met Myra towards the end of his six months in England. A few weeks back in India had convinced him that this was the girl he wanted to marry. Myra had said 'Yes' by long distance telephone and agreed to be married in Madras, rather than waiting for Bob's next home leave.

Young bachelors sent out to India were allowed to marry only after their first tour of duty. When my father went there in the late 1920's, his first tour was for five years. Now, in the 1940's, most people did spells of two-and-a-half years followed by six months' home leave. Even on his second tour, a young man was expected to ask his burra-sahib for permission to marry.

"I hope you've picked a gel who can stand this damned climate," Bob had been told, after permission was duly granted.

The burra-sahib's wife, Auntie Bess as we called her, was holding the reception at her bungalow. She had even suggested the bridesmaids because, apart from Bob, Myra knew not a soul in Madras. It must have been a daunting experience for somebody who had never left England. We had met Myra just twice. She was fair and bouncy, and she had shown us lots of magazines before we had finally chosen the bridesmaids' outfits.

I went now and took off the dress, bringing it carefully back to MK for his final painstaking handwork. MK (the initials stood for two long Tamil names we found hard to pronounce) had been our tailor for as long as I could remember. He wore his shirt tails outside his long white lungi and was never seen without a tape measure around his neck. Jane and I had spent many happy hours sitting beside him, watching as his deft fingers shaped and sewed the material in his lap. He produced all our clothes and a great many of my mother's too. My father went to a different derzi, a man's tailor who worked for a big shop, but MK came to us, sometimes for a month at a time. He made his living by going from house to house, making clothes for Madams and Missies.

"I copy any dress or any picture," he told us. "I make a perfect copy."

When he needed a pattern, he made it himself. But often he would work by drawing in chalk directly onto the material, following the measurements he had taken. These were carefully noted in his little book with symbols known only to himself.

He worked on our back verandah, sitting cross-legged on a white sheet spread over straw mats. To his right, his faithful old Singer sewing machine sat beside him on the floor. It had been given to him by a grateful customer almost twenty years before, when she had bought herself a more up-to-date version in England. Ancient it may have been, but MK could not manage without it. He tended it with loving care and his careful oiling and cleaning paid dividends. On it, he could manage a dress in a few hours.

Sometimes his eldest son came with him to help with the tacking or hemming, particularly if we needed something in a rush. Other times we knew well in advance what we wanted — for instance our fancy dresses for the children's party held each Christmas at the Gymkhana Club. We decided on our costumes weeks ahead and MK would be summoned in good time, because he'd be much in demand around Christmas.

"Have you finished Jennifer Missie's dress?" I asked him about the other bridesmaid. Better than just watching him work was quizzing him about his other customers.

"Yes Missie, all done, and Settle Madam very happy. Not like Randall Madam."

"Why, what's the matter with her?"

"Oh, Randall Madam and Randall Missie having big fight," he said. "Madam always saying Missie must have puffed sleeves."

We all knew that the Randall's daughter was sixteen and, according to conversations overheard between our elders, "growing up fast."

"But Missie not wanting and making big fuss," M.K. continued.

"Why must she have puffed sleeves?" I wanted to know.

"I think Madam wanting Missie to stay little girl, otherwise everybody thinking Madam is too old."

I thought about this pronouncement and later asked my mother whether MK could be right.

"Quite likely," she said. "Mrs. Randall has been thirty-five for several years now." She wrinkled her forehead. "I must ring Bess and check what time she wants us to be at the Fort tomorrow." The marriage ceremony was to be held there, in St. Mary's Church, the fashionable place for a Protestant wedding in Madras. I returned to the back verandah.

"Don't come on the sheet with your shoes on," warned Jane.

"I won't make it dirty because I haven't been anywhere," I answered. "These are my new shoes for tomorrow and I'm getting used to them."

I resumed my cross-legged position beside MK. Occasionally he'd give us odd pieces of material and let us use his marking wheel, but never his massive scissors. "Too dangerous, Missies," he would say, "and I'm needing to keep them very sharp."

He was chewing on a little ball of thread because he had a habit of popping any thread ends into his mouth rather than leaving them to lie around. When the collection became too big, he would go to the edge of the verandah and spit it out. Like his cutting out scissors, his teeth too needed to be sharp because he always used them to bite off the sewing cotton.

Almost every day MK's wife, Akiah, brought his lunch. She carried it in a tiffin carrier, a useful contraption where each aluminium dish fitted onto the one below and was stacked into a cylindrical metal container onto which was clipped a lid with a handle. It was amazing how warm the food stayed. In her bright cotton sari, Akiah would squat on her haunches beside him and unload a dish of rice followed by pungent curries and dhal. She would proffer us little mounds on the lid.

"Try Missies, try," she would urge us in Tamil.

Knowing that we must use only the fingers of our right hand, because the left is reserved for more unhygienic tasks like washing instead of using toilet paper, we tried surreptitiously. Depriving the servants of their food was forbidden, but it always smelled and tasted so much better than our own lunch.

'It must be almost lunch time now,' I thought, and began watching out for Akiah. When she appeared, carrying not only the tiffin carrier, but a bundle, and on her hip their youngest child, I jumped up to help her. The slippery soles of my new shoes slid on the verandah steps. I landed in a heap at the bottom, one foot twisted up under me. Jane was beside me in seconds. The pain, when she tried to pull me up, was excruciating

"Ouch," I yelped. "Call Mummy quickly."

The doctor came and diagnosed a sprained ankle. "You won't be walking on that for a while, young lady," he said. "We'll have to find you a pair of crutches."

"But I can't be a bridesmaid with crutches," I wailed.

There was a lot of frantic telephoning and finally the decision was made. It was not one that made me happy, but I supposed things could have been worse. Jane would take my place at the wedding.

In his little book M.K. found the page with her measurements. My beautiful dress was unpicked at the waist, and by early evening it fitted her perfectly.

"You will have to wear your dancing pumps," my mother told her. "We haven't got time to get new shoes made."

"I wouldn't wear them," said Jane, looking pointedly at my bandaged leg. "And I don't want to wear the necklace either. It's Anne's."

"Both bridesmaids are supposed to wear the same," I told her, secretly pleased at her gesture. Jennifer and I had been given our bridesmaids' presents in advance, so that we could wear them at the wedding.

The next day, I fingered the gold chain interspersed with tiny pearls, as I sat waiting in the church. The flower arrangements were of pink and white carnations, whose scent vied with the dusty, musky smell of the old building.

"We'll put you on the bride's side," the ushers in their morning suits told my parents. Behind them, I hopped my way up the aisle on my crutches.

Jane was waiting with Jennifer at the main church door. St. Mary's also has doors down both sides leading out to wide verandahs, which shaded the massively thick walls. Even centuries ago, they had known how to build for coolness. It did not occur to me to wonder how many thousands of English brides had begun new lives in this church. I was more intrigued by the punkahs or old fans, which I knew had once been operated by small boys pulling on the ropes. When their arms got tired, they were supposed to have tied the ropes to their toes and kept the punkahs moving with their legs. I'd have liked to have seen that.

In the cool quietness of the church, we listened to the whirring of the modern electric fans hanging from the ceiling. The bells had stopped peeling some minutes before and suddenly, into the languid afternoon, the organ burst forth with the opening bars of 'Here comes the Bride'.

I turned to look at Myra in her white dress and long veil. I liked her and, in the words of the man on whose arm she walked, I hoped she could "stand this damned climate". Certainly she looked cool now — and beautiful. I looked behind her to my sister. She looked lovely too. Well, pink always was Jane's favourite colour, I thought. I resolved there and then that my first long evening dress would be …green. And it certainly wouldn't have puffed sleeves!

CHAPTER SIX

THE SCHOOL IN A HILL STATION

Finally, the time came for Jane and me to go to boarding school. In February 1950, we arrived at St. Hilda's, the missionary school in Ootacamund that our parents had chosen. There were only about fifty pupils and I was surprised to discover that, at twelve, I was one of the oldest there. There were five of us in the top form; we were known as the 'A's and remained the most senior until we left at sixteen or seventeen. It meant that our tenure as head girl or house captains lasted all that time, and probably resulted in our being very bossy.

The experience of being a boarder at a small school in an Indian hill station was so totally different to being a day girl at a large public school in England. For a start, I soon knew every pupil in the school and, as one of the two house captains, was expected to encourage the younger ones to earn 'stars' for good marks or behaviour. These were added up each week and there was intense rivalry between the Houses as to who would earn the most. Homework was done at a set time each evening, between supper and bedtime, and occasionally our lessons were held out of doors.

Our headmistress, Miss Hall, liked her pupils to spend as much time in the open air as possible, and was prone to sitting us 'A's down on a grassy bank in the sunshine, where she lectured us on English grammar or Latin verbs.

As well as being an Anglican missionary, she had graduated from Oxford University with an Honours degree, was an excellent teacher and held our attention despite the unorthodox surroundings. I remember particularly her ability to impart knowledge and idealism when she gave me, and three others, lessons before our Confirmation into the Christian faith at the age of fourteen.

When one year the Aurora Borealis became visible, an exception in India, Miss Hall had the whole school out of their classrooms and on the playground to admire this beautiful display of nature. Another year, her sense of humour manifested itself when she played an April Fool's joke on us. When the bell rang to summon us to breakfast, we all rushed out of our dormitories to another building, which housed the dining room. Unusually, the door was locked and we could not get in. Eventually the whole school was crowded outside, and still no teachers appeared to tell us what had happened. With stomachs rumbling with hunger, we were kept waiting a quarter-of-an-hour until Miss Hall appeared and began lecturing us on our behaviour, which warranted the punishment of no breakfast. We were stupefied, not knowing what we had done. At the end of her speech the door was suddenly opened by our Deputy Headmistress, who pronounced us all April Fools.

Our teachers were Anglican missionaries, English, Canadian and Belgian, and after breakfast and supper each day, we all filed into the tiny chapel to pray and sing a hymn. Even the pupils of other religions attended, although I think they could have refused to do so. There were several Hindu and Muslim girls amongst us, and one or two I have met in later life have said that they were glad to have undergone the experience.

Late afternoon, on weekdays, we often played netball, and again there was great rivalry between the two Houses. We united, however, to put forward our best team to play schools in the surrounding area. Of these there were several, as the climate of the Nilgiri Hills was considered to be far more beneficial for children's health than the heat of the Plains below (ie. sea level).

Sometimes on weekends, we went on picnics. We piled into the school bus with a teacher or two and were driven into the countryside; sometimes to waterfalls, sometimes to Doddabetta, which at 8,606 feet, is the highest peak in the Nilgiris. At one of our picnic spots there was a stream, and I always wanted to swim in it. This activity was strictly forbidden, but occasionally somebody fell in trying to catch tadpoles. She would be bundled into the bus and wrapped in a rug, because the temperature in the Nilgiris was quite cool, reminding people of an English spring. We sat on the grass and ate sausage rolls and jam sandwiches before being allowed to wander off and explore. There was always the possibility that we might meet a snake, if not a wild animal, and we were told not to go far and to return as soon as we heard a blast on the whistle.

Jane and I found school much more fun than it had ever been in England. Nevertheless, we looked forward to the time our mother would come to the Hills for the Hot Weather, and we could spend the weekends with her.

Makinah House

My fourteenth birthday party in the Makinah House garden
with Ayah, far left, and the Major, far right

When my mother came to Ooty, as Ootacamund was
commonly known, she always stayed at Makinah House.
This was a collection of small apartments, which could
be rented for short periods, and provided an income for a
certain crusty old major, who had retired from the Indian
Army and made Ooty his home. He'd cultivated a pretty
garden with all the flowers one would find in an English
herbaceous border. They thrived in the climate of the hill

station, although they might not have done in the hot Plains below. He had provided a swing seat and rattan chairs for all the residents to use, and was often to be found sitting out there smoking.

The apartment my mother rented was just big enough for us to come out from school for the weekend, but when my father came up for a few days, I was demoted to a camp bed on the enclosed verandah. Ayah, who accompanied my mother wherever she went, then had to sleep on the floor. This was nothing unusual for her as, in Madras, she liked to sleep on a mat next to my little sister's bed, perhaps to get the benefit of the overhead fan. In her cramped and hot godown at the back of the house, there was only room for one chapoi (bed with a wooden frame and webbing) and this was occupied by her old mother, who lived with her.

All our other servants remained in Madras to look after the house and my father as he toiled in the sweltering Hot Weather, with just a few days off to visit us in Ooty. So, apart from Ayah, the only other servant we had at Makinah House was a cook/bearer, whom my mother employed with references from the Major. As only my mother and Sue were there during the week, and Ayah made beds and dusted, his duties were not very onerous. At the weekends, however, we came home from school and demanded all our favourite dishes, which the poor man could never produce as well as our dear Cookie in Madras.

Occasionally we went out for a Chinese meal, but our favourite jaunt was down to Charing Cross, Ooty's busy shopping area, where we scoffed coffee ice cream in Kwality's. As I remember from my very early days,

Ooty did once have a café/tea room, which was owned by a Frenchman and served the most delicious cream cakes. Unfortunately, by the time I went to school, it had closed and we had to rely on our own and the school's cooks for birthday cakes.

Activities on our weekends out from school included visits to Ooty's lake, where rowing boats could be hired, and Jane and I took turns with the oars while trying not to run us aground. We went shopping at Spencer's, a mini version of the large store in Madras, which sold everything from bacon to beauty products. The Assembly Rooms was a theatre and cinema in town, which only rarely had live shows, except when one of the schools put on a production. It did though show English films, which we went to see whenever a Hollywood musical came to town, because my mother knew how much we enjoyed the song and dance routines.

Sometimes we went with my mother to the Golf Club and walked the course with her, or coaxed some of her friends into playing Canasta with us in the Clubhouse. I don't know whether children were not allowed into the renowned Ooty Club, but I don't remember being taken there until the year I was seventeen. That year I was allowed, on my birthday, to go to a dance which the Ooty Club held most Saturdays during the Season; ie. the months of April and May, when the town was crowded with visitors escaping the hot weather in the Plains. These months were filled with gaiety at dances and dinner parties. There were Flower and Dog Shows, horse racing and point-to-points, as well as hunting and golf. Sometimes, husbands would join their wives on a fortnight's holiday, and numbers were swelled by army officers on leave from their regiments in other parts of India leading, it was rumoured, to innumerable scandalous liaisons.

For the Hot Weather, the Governor of Madras brought his entourage to Government House set in the magnificent botanical Government Gardens. In the latter, there are many different species of trees and flowers, and it is open for the public to roam around. In contrast, the Ooty Club was available only to members, who had been carefully selected, and their guests. Black tie was essential for the dances, and the band played at one end of the vast ballroom, whose walls were adorned with numerous antlers and a tiger's head. As far as I know, these remain as the Club's decorations to this day, together with photographs of long-dead Masters of Foxhounds in the large austere dining room. In the bar, wooden plaques embossed in gold announce the names of winners of point-to-point races first held decades ago, and in the Secretary's office albums show photographs of revelling Club members long vanished.

I was not of course allowed in the Billiards Room, a Men Only sanctuary, which the Club claims is the birthplace of Snooker. In fact, the game was invented by Colonel Sir Neville Chamberlain (not the Prime Minister but another Sir Neville) in 1875, while serving in the army in Jubbulpore. After being wounded in the Afghan War, he moved to Ooty, where the rules of Snooker were finally drawn up and posted in the Ooty Club's Billiards Room.

I was, however, allowed in the Club's bar, although I spent most of my time on the dance floor, because

Saturday nights was when young planters from the surrounding tea estates interrupted their lonely lives with a visit to the Ooty Club.

EASTER AT SCHOOL

When Easter fell early in the year and my mother had not yet arrived from Madras, we spent the short break at school. Our teachers, being missionaries, made sure we embraced the religious aspect of the holiday and, as on every other day, we went to the little school chapel to pray every morning and evening. The difference was that on Easter Day the chapel was filled with flowers to celebrate the Rising of Christ from the dead. Armfuls of blooms were brought in on Easter Saturday, and the more senior girls were allowed to try their hands at flower arranging.

On Easter Sunday, as on other Sundays, the whole school trooped down to Ooty town to attend the service at St. Stephen's Church. Consecrated in 1831, this stood in a graveyard filled with tombs bearing the names of generations of Britons who had given their lives for the Raj. Especially at Easter, there was an abundance of flowers in the church, and a packed congregation in their Sunday best. Extravagant hats and brilliant saris added to the colourful scene. We school children wore our uniform of grey skirt and jacket with a cornflower blue shirt. The younger children were seated at the back, from where they could be ushered out before the sermon began. They were deemed incapable of sitting still long enough to listen to its end.

Usually a teacher went with them, but sometimes it fell to one of us senior girls to supervise their antics in the graveyard until the end of the service. It was hard to ignore the sad stories told by the graves of a 'beloved young wife lost in childbirth', or a three-year old child 'stolen by small-pox', or a 'much loved husband taken by cholera'. During the time that I was there, tropical diseases had mostly been eradicated due to advances in medical science. Cholera, smallpox, malaria, diphtheria and other tropical diseases, which had so decimated the forces of the Raj, were almost entirely wiped out.

The climb back to school, even by 'the shortcut', a mud-packed winding path, was arduous, and we were all pleased to sit down to the special Easter lunch that awaited us. After lunch we were normally allowed to go to our tuck boxes, which were kept in a cupboard outside the dining room, and were supposed to take out just two or three sweets. Easter time was different. Our parents could send us Easter eggs, which they did in quantity, size and variety, and we could gorge ourselves until we were sick.

One Easter I really was sick, not with chocolate, but with mumps. I must have had a strong immune system because, as with any epidemic raging through the school, I was one of the last to succumb. Only five of us were stuck in the sick room with our swellings and Easter parcels, trying with aching jaws to get our teeth into all the choco-late eggs our parents had posted to us. It was a truly painful time and we envied the rest of the school, who were being taken on a picnic on Easter Monday. We didn't feel like trying some of the tricks we sometimes employed to get us out of the sick-room, such as drinking cold water just before Matron came round with her thermometer.

To add to our discomfort, we had to share a bathroom where our five thunder-boxes (commodes) were placed in a row, and we no longer had the privacy we normally enjoyed when each one was in a cubicle assigned, at least for the older girls, to an individual alone. There was no plumbed sanitation at the school, and men were employed to empty the thunder-boxes at regular intervals throughout the day. The bathrooms of most big old houses in India had back doors to facilitate this unpleasant job in the days before drainage to cess pits and sewers became customary.

The school's bathing arrangements were equally archaic. Tin baths were placed in cubicles into which the waterman poured about four inches of scalding water that he'd heated up on a brazier outside. Each girl had then to run enough cold water into a bucket to bring her bath to a temperature she found comfortable. Fortunately, the one tap providing water for this was inside the communal washroom.

We older girls were pleased that we had our baths in the evening, after sweaty games of netball, when we were allowed to change from our uniforms into home clothes for supper. The mornings were always a rush, especially if you did not get out of bed the minute the bell rang, because it was a rule that we make our beds before breakfast. At home I never made my own bed, believing that to be Ayah's job, and also that my shoes would be cleaned for me. Matron, however, insisted that we polish our shoes to an impeccable shine and I regret to say that I sometimes coaxed my sister

Jane to do mine for me.

The boys, who could attend the school up to the age of nine or ten, had their own Matron, whom we all called 'Nursie'. There were only about a dozen boys, and they had their own dormitories on the other side of the main building, which housed the dining room and the gymnasium. Although a number of pupils were Indian, they were all expected to follow the Church of England teachings and the English curriculum, after which we took the Senior Cambridge School Certificate. Some of the Muslim girls did have extra lessons from a Munshi (teacher), who came in and gave them tuition in Urdu and probably the teachings of the Koran.

Moti and the Gymkhana Races

One of the extra-curricular activities our parents chose for us was riding, and falling off Moti was something I did regularly. Moti was a chestnut hill pony or 'tat' pony, a breed found in the Nilgiri Hills in South India. He was a stallion who supposedly had been gelded, although the procedure appeared not to have worked properly. He was temperamental and bucked and neighed a lot, but his syce who was both groom and owner, had managed to persuade Miss Scott, our riding instructor, that he was a suitable mount for one of her pupils and should be hired on a regular basis. This situation was the ambition of all the syces who owned ponies in Ooty. It meant a regular income and, though a motley crowd themselves, they groomed their ponies to catch her eye.

As I was the oldest, though not the most competent of her pupils, I was assigned to ride Moti. My most spectacular fall occurred when, bringing up the rear of our group of eight, I managed to keep one foot caught in a stirrup and was dragged along the ground for two or three yards. Fortunately I was not hurt, but it was with great trepidation that I obeyed the order to mount him again and carry on.

Moti's syce was called Swami and he, together with the other ponies' syces, had been ambling along behind us on the forest path. Now he tried to reassure me.

"Moti not bucking again, Missie. He seeing something in the trees. I lead him now."

On another occasion he told me. "Moti very good pony — he winning many Gymkhana races."

This I could believe. When we had been told to canter gently across the Downs, as the rolling green hills around Ooty are known, he'd bolted with me and galloped so fast that I had no hope of pulling him up.

Sometimes, when riding on the Downs, we came across groups of Todas. They are a hill tribe indigenous to the Nilgiris and keep themselves very much to themselves. They wear shawls with borders of brightly coloured stripes and don't cut their hair. They graze their cattle, mostly buffaloes, on the Downs and lived in houses of mud and thatch shaped rather like igloos forming a point at the top with a hole for the smoke to come out. The only other opening and the way into the hut was via a tiny curved door through which they almost had to crawl. We would have loved to have looked inside, but it was obvious that they wanted to keep their distance and so we rode on past their little settlements.

The Downs were where people played golf and where the Ooty Hunt met. The pack of hounds was carefully nurtured, the Master of the Hunt wore pink, and each Meet began with the traditional stirrup cup. The only difference from a Meet in England was that foxes were not hunted but jackals. These were considered dangerous and a pest by the locals. We found their howling, which we sometimes heard at night when lying in bed at school, quite scary. Miss Scott was a staunch supporter of the Ooty Hunt, a long-time Ooty resident and much admired for her horsemanship. She usually rode a grey mare called Lancelette, which my sister Jane, probably the most competent rider in our group, was occasionally allowed to mount. Miss Scott and Lancelette took part in point-to-points and, at the Gymkhana Races, competed in the Ladies Race, which she often won. The Gymkhana Races were held at the race course at the end of the main flat racing season. Most of the races were for the local hill (tat) ponies, which were ridden by their owners, and there was great rivalry between the syces of the ponies we rode under Miss Scott's supervision.

One day we had mounted our ponies and were standing around waiting for Miss Scott, when Jane suddenly announced, "Anand says my pony is going to win the big race at the Gymkhana Races."

"Of course he won't. Moti will win it," I replied.

"I hope Rocket and Anand win because his wife has just had a baby, and they need the money," she retorted.

Miss Scott arrived.

"Stop chattering girls," she ordered. "We're going to concentrate on the rising trot today. I don't want you bobbing about like a lot of corks on an ocean wave."

"Do you think Moti will beat Rocket in the big race on Saturday?" I asked her.

"Most probably," she answered. "Now come on."

The day of the big race came. My mother was up in Ooty, so we were out of school for the weekend and could go to the races. My mother took her spare binoculars for us to share and bought us race cards. For us, the third race was the important one.

"I'm going to bet on Anand," Jane proclaimed.

That morning, we'd been given pocket money and were allowed to bet on the Tote.

"You're wasting your money," I told her. "He has no hope of beating Swami and Moti."

"I'm not betting on anything," said my little sister Sue, "but I might bet on Miss Scott when she rides in a race."

"She is not riding today, darling," my mother told her. "You're quite right to save your money."

We watched the ponies in the paddock. Of course our syces had no silks, so I tried to make a mental note of what shirts they were wearing. I would certainly remember that Swami was wearing a green one and Anand a red and blue check. Moti did some neighing in the paddock but was otherwise perfectly behaved. They cantered down to the start.

There were fifteen runners altogether and it was a seven-furlong race. The flag went down and they were off. Both Moti and Rocket got away to a good start and Moti soon hit the front.

"Let me see, let me see," demanded Jane, and grabbed the binoculars from me. "At the moment Rocket is third, but not very far behind," she commentated excitedly.

"Wait till they come round the bend," I countered. "Moti will pull right away then."

The ponies were all bunched together with Moti still in the lead. As they came into the straight I took hold of the binoculars again. Something strange was happening. The green shirt was no longer in front. There was an excited shout from Jane.

"Rocket has taken the lead."

I looked again and couldn't believe my eyes. Swami had dropped to the back and was pulling Moti up.

"He's gone lame," said my mother. "He has dropped right out."

"Come on Rocket," shouted Jane, and almost as though he had heard, 'her' pony made a final spurt and crossed the finishing line a good length ahead of the others. Jane was exultant.

"I told you," she said. "Anand said he was going to win."

Poor Moti limped home and it was several weeks before I was given the dubious pleasure of riding him again, but I am sure that Anand and his family flourished on the big prize money.

CHAPTER SEVEN

A TREAT BUT NO TIGER

One year my parents had several winning horses at the
Madras Races. They decided, as a treat, to fly Jane and
me home for the short half-term holiday at Easter. The
journey, about 335 miles, normally took seventeen hours
and involved an overnight train. We usually made it in a
large group accompanied by teachers at the beginning and
end of term, but never for half term and certainly not on
our own. But our kind and accommodating headmistress,
Miss Hall, worked out a plan. She and the deputy headmistress would drive Jane and me from Ootacamund to
Coimbatore in 'the Plains' (i.e. sea level), and put us on
an Indian Airlines flight, which my parents would meet in
Madras. We were extremely excited, both at the prospect of
going home, which we had not expected to do for another
two months, and also about flying in an aeroplane, which
we had never done before.

"Do you think I'll be sick?" Jane asked.

She was known for being sick on any boat, even the
stabilised liners that took us to England and back.

"Only if there's a big storm," I replied, trying to be the
reassuring big sister and not knowing a thing about airline
travel. Little did I realise that the journey by car down the
Ghat road, from 7,350 feet to sea level, would be more
nausea-inducing than the plane journey.

On the Wednesday before Good Friday we climbed

into Miss Hall's little car, dressed so we could readily shed garments as we progressed down the mountainside until we reached the scorching heat of Coimbatore in April. Jane and I were installed in the back and found the first three or four hairpin bends exhilarating, but the novelty soon began to wane. Round and down we went, again and again, sometimes with fantastic views of the Plains, misty mauve in the distance; sometimes passing roadside stalls selling fruit, snacks and beedis, the poor man's cigarettes; and mostly through forests of trees close to the edge of the road. There were monkeys in profusion, some just sitting to watch us and a few darting across the road in front of us.

"Look out for other animals," said Miss Hall. "You might see an elephant, and if we're lucky, we could see a tiger."

On the narrow road, lorries passed us with little room to spare, slowly grinding up the inclines in first gear. To our great disappointment, we drove out of tiger country without spotting one, and as we reached the lower slopes the vegetation changed, palm trees began to appear, and people and habitations became more numerous. From the clear spring-like air of a hill station, we were back in the heat, dust and smells of the India I will always associate with my happiest childhood days.

At Coimbatore airport, Miss Hall handed us over to the airline authorities, who had been informed that two minors would be travelling on the flight to Madras.

"Have a happy Easter," she said, "and we'll see you again next week."

A smartly uniformed official took charge of us. We

had only hand luggage and there were few formalities; just the checking of our names against a list, and then we were led out to the waiting plane. An air hostess came to show us how to fasten our seat belts and told us we only had to wear them for take-off and landing. She said nothing about wearing them in turbulence, which was probably just as well, because I was now beginning to feel nervous as well as excited. The engines began to rev, and Jane and I held hands as the little Fokker Friendship raced down the runway and took off effortlessly into the sky.

When Coimbatore had vanished below the clouds, our pretty hostess brought us orange juice and biscuits.

"When we go down to land," she said, "don't get worried if you feel the plane bump. It's only the wheels hitting the ground and the pilot doesn't always manage to avoid it."

Not long afterwards we were descending and, as the sprawl of Madras city appeared, we tried to make out landmarks, especially the rivers because one of them, the Cooum, flowed near our house. Then we were down with a bump and taxiing along the runway.

When the landing steps were in place, Jane and I were among the first out of the door. We ran across the tarmac and into our parents' arms. We hugged our little sister Sue, who at four was too young to go to boarding school. It was great to be home. Back at the bungalow, Ayah and Kanaan were on the front verandah waiting for us. The dog barked with excitement and even our very own tiger, a stuffed head and skin, which lay as a rug on the sitting room floor, seemed to say 'welcome home'.

Of all the things we liked to do on holiday, our favourite was to go swimming, and this we did almost every day of this Easter break, either in the pool at the Gymkhana Club or in the sea. With the temperatures reaching 110°F, it was a pleasant relief to slip into the water, and we could understand why this time of the year was known as 'the Hot Weather'. Many wives with their young children, left their husbands at work in the Plains while they decamped to the hill stations for several months, and to avoid the heat, older children were sent to boarding schools in the hill stations. The principal hill station for Madras was Ootacamund, considered Queen of the Hill Stations in South India and known as 'Snooty Ooty', because it was where the Governor of the Presidency (after 1947 of the State of Madras which only became Tamil Nadu in 1969) and his entourage moved to every Hot Weather. My mother went to Ooty every April and May, and then again in September, so this year she, Sue and Ayah would accompany us back to school on the train.

I was a little disappointed that we would be unable to do more tiger spotting. The little hill train always chugged too noisily up the mountainside, emitting loud whistles rounding corners to warn off people and animals on the line. I told my mother about our unfulfilled hopes for a tiger on the Ghat road. She suggested a trip to the zoo.

"I don't know whether they'll have a tiger," she said, "but they are bound to have some of the large cats — maybe a panther or a leopard."

We went on Easter Saturday afternoon. Little Sue was excited and kept asking if we would see an elephant. To her delight there was a big elephant and an adorable baby one there. But there was no tiger. We watched a panther climb a tree and I was fascinated by the elegance of a sinewy leopard prowling around. Jane wanted to spend longer watching the haughty giraffes. In the Reptile House, we were educated about the snakes we might find in our compound.

Back home, I asked my father about the rug in the sitting room.

"Daddy, did you shoot our tiger?"

"No," he said. "I bought him already stuffed from Ian, a tea planter, when he retired. The tiger was terrifying his workers, prowling around their village at night, and eventually killed a cow. Ian sat in a tree with his gun all one night and managed to shoot him dead."

On Easter Sunday our parents organised an Easter egg hunt. This took place inside the bungalow because of the dangers outdoors. They didn't want us ferreting around the garden, where there was always the danger we might step on a snake or put our hands on a scorpion. Jane and I were instructed not to find the egg hidden in the open jaws of the tiger because that was a place easy for little Sue to find. In the end, she found just as many eggs as we did, probably due to her big sisters from time to time pointing her in the right direction.

The next evening we had to catch the train to Ooty. As we drove to Madras Central Station, I reflected on our holiday. It had indeed been a special treat, and my only regret was that we had not seen a live tiger.

GUY FAWKES NIGHT

At St. Hilda's, we always celebrated Guy Fawkes Night. This was because the 5th November was the birthday of the son of our Deputy Headmistress. The school took boys up to the age of nine or ten, and their dormitories were in a separate annexe to ours, but Johnnie lived with his mother, also on the premises, and was rather envied by us, who thought he got away with a lot of mischief. But we did appreciate his birthday party, when we had a huge bonfire and fireworks. Johnnie's mother, who also looked after household matters, made the most delicious mocha cream birthday cake, which we ate later; grilled sausages were served around the fire; and we older girls were allowed to bake potatoes in the embers.

For weeks beforehand, the whole school collected wood for the bonfire. It made our compulsory walks much more fun, and even the youngest brought back bundles of sticks, often tied together with our mackintosh belts if we'd forgotten to take any rope. Our walks led us through eucalyptus trees, whose scent hung heavily in the air. It is perhaps the blue-green colour of their leaves that gives the Nilgiri Hills their alternative name of the Blue Mountains. The woods could be quite dense and we always thought there was the chance of seeing a tiger, particularly if we had heard rumours that a man-eater had attacked cattle in one of the servants' nearby villages.

One year, the 'A's decided that we would make a special guy for the bonfire, and that the rest of the school would have no sight of him until we triumphantly produced him on the 5th November. This meant that we needed a secret place, where our handiwork would not be seen by the other pupils. Matron had two young assistants, both of whom we called 'Nurse' although they were not trained nurses, and we persuaded one of them to let us work in her room. She always kept her door locked so nobody else would go in there, and she let us have a key.

Our next problem was finding the material from which to concoct a Guy. We had access to straw with which to stuff him and, for his body we salvaged a sack in which the kitchen staff had received vegetables. The problem was his arms and legs. Then one of us had a brilliant idea. She had an old pair of pyjamas that were wearing out; she would donate them to be stuffed for arms and legs, and would write home for a new pair! Guy's head was easy as Johnnie's mother gave us an old pillowcase, which we fashioned into shape and adorned with a carrot for a nose after drawing on eyes and mouth. Although Nurse was not too happy with the straw in her bedroom, she was a real sport about it and kept our secret till the end.

By November 5th, our bonfire had grown to quite a height, so when we brought the Guy down amid the *oohs* and *aahs* of the assembled pupils, we had difficulty getting him to the top. Finally, he was in place and Miss Hall, our Headmistress, set fire to the whole edifice with the help of Ramaswami, the head bearer, and rags soaked in paraffin. Slowly, the flames took hold and the air was filled with the smell of burning eucalyptus wood. As darkness fell, I looked out from our vantage point high above the town and saw the lights of Ooty twinkling below us. The air was chill and the warmth of the bonfire behind was comforting. 7,500 feet below, at the bottom of the Ghat road, which snaked in a series of hairpin bends, lay the Plains. I remembered the different kind of warmth that enveloped us there and looked forward to the end of term.

The 'A's with Guy Fawkes. From left: Ann Livy, myself, Durr, Suzanne, Dee

I collected a potato to bake. "Please Anne, will you bake this one for me?" asked Ranjini, a classmate of Jane's. "It will take quite a time," I answered her. "It may not be ready until after the fireworks." We were not allowed near the fireworks, which Miss Hall was setting up, but Johnnie's mother was handing out sparklers to the younger pupils. Suddenly, a rocket zoomed high into the dark night sky and shattered into a myriad of falling stars. Johnnie's birthday celebration had begun.

When the last firework had lit up the sky, we were told to go over and wait in the hall outside the dining room.

"Tonight we'll say grace there," said Miss Hall, "and not at the tables as we usually do."

"Yes," piped up Johnnie, "because once you get inside, you've got to find your places. I've had Mum put out little cards so that everybody has to sit next to their worst enemies, or it might even be their best friends as it's my birthday party."

"In other words," said his mother, "you can all sit exactly where you like, and not divided up with one from each form at each table, as usual."

"But," said Miss Hall, "I think you 'A' form girls had better each take a table to keep order, as everybody seems so excited."

We sampled sandwiches of egg, tomato and cucumber. Then the sausage rolls were brought in, and finally the large mocha cream birthday cake, ablaze with candles for Johnnie to blow out, as we all sang "Happy Birthday". The cake was delicious and several more were produced so that everybody could have a large slice.

The next day, when I thanked Johnnie's mother for a lovely party, she told me, "I know you may all think Johnnie is a spoilt child and that he comes running to me with tales about you, but he never tells me things which he thinks might get any of you children into trouble. He just wants to be accepted as one of you."

HOME FOR THE HOLIDAYS

The sight of luscious green paddy fields flashing by filled me with sheer joy. Because my sister Jane and I were going home for the holidays, I always felt like this as the train from Mettupalayam sped through the villages on the outskirts of Madras. It took two trains, including an overnight journey, to reach home from our school in Ooty in the Nilgiri Hills. Adults may have liked the cool of the hill station, but we children preferred the heat and brilliant sunshine of the Plains, and the glory of a Jacaranda tree in full bloom to the smell of Eucalyptus trees.

We arrived at Madras Central Station early in the morning. On the platform, along with many other parents, were my father, mother and youngest sister Sue. Joseph, our driver, took us all home, while the trunks and bedding rolls followed on bullock carts, accompanied by our water-man, Munswami.

On the front verandah of our house, our servants were waiting to greet us. It was time for breakfast, our first meal at home for a couple of months, and one we always anticipated with relish. There were mangos and papayas, bacon and eggs — and toast.

"We don't get toast at school," said Jane, "only bread and butter. But we do get mangos, and we make them into guinea-pigs".

I had to explain. "First we suck all the fruit off the mango stones. Then we wash them and scrub them clean with our nail brushes. When they are dry, some of them have quite long hair, so we cover them in talcum powder, comb them and make an eye either side with our pens. Last term it was quite a craze."

"So I suppose there were lots of little girls running around with guinea-pigs in their pockets," laughed my mother.

Then Jane piped up. "Couldn't we have a real guinea pig as a pet?"

"No," said my father. "We're getting something far more exciting than that. I'm having a hundred day-old chicks flown out from England, and it will be quite a job to keep them alive and grow them up."

My father had the idea that poultry stock in India needed improving. Instead of the scrawny chickens usually found there, he wanted plump Rhode Island Reds like those he knew back home in England.

Our mali made sturdy wooden pens with wire netting stretched over them to house the expected arrivals. These were necessary to keep out any snakes or marauding animals like bandicoots, grey squirrels and mongooses, but especially to protect the chicks from kites, which could swoop down from the skies and carry off the tiny birds.

A few days later, we went to the airport to collect the chicks. With great excitement, we took the five boxes home and opened them to find a mass of yellow fluff huddling together. Amazingly, only six had not survived the long flight from London. Almost two days old, we found them adorable as we cradled them in our palms. Sue had to be prompted not to squeeze them when they squirmed in her little hands. The chicks were put into the pens under the guava trees in the garden. They were hungry and thirsty, and pecked feverishly at the grain we strewed on the ground for them.

From then on, we ran out early every morning to make sure they were still alive. We already had hens in a chicken run and were used to collecting the eggs whenever we heard a chicken cackling outside. We had had baby chicks before, because Kanaan sometimes put a broody hen to sit on a clutch of eggs in the little room next to the kitchen that was his storeroom, but never had the chicks seemed as precious as these which had travelled so many thousands of miles.

Kanaan was entranced. He had adopted my father's interest in poultry and ensured that the chicken house and run were kept repaired. He was good at organising his team, except of course Ayah, and arranged much of our fun, like swings and the building of our tree houses. Half way down our drive and placed on either side of it were two trees with spreading branches. Planks were tied into them, where Jane and I each sat and surveyed the comings and goings, not just of our visitors, but those of our servants, their children, and the family who lived upstairs. Our holidays were never boring. We swam almost every morning, and often played tennis in the afternoon, but only after 4 p.m. when the sun was not beating down so harshly. Then, this holiday, we had the chicks to keep an eye on. They were eating and growing well.

One morning we went outside early and found, to our horror, that eight of them were lying still on the ground. We ran inside.

"Daddy, come quickly! Something has happened to

the chicks."

After his inspection, my father confirmed that they were dead, and quite a few more were huddled droopily in a corner.

"We've got to call the vet straight away" he said. "We don't want any more dying, and we had better move the droopy ones into a pen on their own. It may be something contagious."

The pens were all moved to fresh ground, and the poor little dead chicks were taken away to be buried. Sue was in tears.

The vet arrived and told my father that the most likely cause was a disease to which poultry in India were prone, and that we could lose the whole lot. He prescribed medication to go in their water, and told us to continue to separate any more that appeared sick. It was a worrying time and we checked constantly, only to find two or three more dead each day. My father called the vet again, who said there was nothing more he could do, and we must wait for the medication to work. After a week, we went out one morning and found that all the remaining chicks were still alive. They began to look more and more perky, and by the end of the holidays we had fifty-five almost fully-grown Rhode Island Reds to feed. They were certainly more interesting than a guinea-pig, and we were grateful that we had managed to save so many.

OUR LOVED AND LOYAL SERVANTS

Ayah, as a staunch Catholic who had been educated by missionaries, often read us Bible stories. One Christmas she'd saved up to buy us a beautifully illustrated book of parables for children. Another year, when we were older, she asked my mother for special permission to take Jane and me to Midnight Mass on Christmas Eve.

We were used to seeing her in a white sari, but on this occasion she had chosen a brilliant blue one with a silver border. Her youngest daughter, Esther, came with us. She wore fragrant jasmine in her hair, which she had coated with coconut oil and braided into a thick plait. For us all, it was a special occasion.

The church was packed with both Indians and Europeans. As Protestants, Jane and I were not used to a Catholic Mass and were fascinated by the rituals of wafting incense and sprinkling holy water. We sat quietly while Ayah and Esther took Communion, except for the occasional whispered comment on somebody's attire. Then we all streamed out into the dark humid night. My mother had given Ayah money to pay for a taxi home but, with the crowd, it was impossible to find one. So Esther and I climbed into one cycle rickshaw with Ayah and Jane in another, and we arrived home knowing that we would not get much sleep before our little sister Sue woke us with excited exclamations over her Christmas stocking.

It was not usual to employ servants of different religions in a household, and to keep the peace, the mixing of Hindus and Muslims was avoided. Certainly, having a Christian Ayah and a Hindu bearer led occasionally to friction in our house. Ayah thought herself superior to any Hindu and would take no orders from Kanaan, our bearer. She also considered herself equal to the Eurasian/ Anglo-Indian nannies whom many memsahibs employed, probably for snob value, but also, somewhat for safety. These nannies were unlikely to indulge in odd practices like putting kerosene in a child's hair to get rid of nits, or administering opium to get a child to sleep.

Some of the Hindu practices we witnessed and enjoyed took place at festival times. At Pongal, cows, secretly tethered at the back of our compound so no one would be incensed by the curtailment of their liberty, had their horns painted in bright colours. At Diwali, little earthenware dishes with wicks soaked in oil would be set alight outside the servants' godowns. Our nearby bazaar, which was called Thousand Lights Bazaar, looked spectacular with these dishes placed all along the side of the road.

We occasionally went to the Bazaar with Ayah if she had not had time during the day to get herself something for supper. She would buy a few vegetables, maybe some spices, from a gnarled old woman with her wares laid out on a cloth on the ground; sometimes from a more established stall holder or a little shop. There was always such hustle and bustle and the vendors would make a big fuss of 'Little Missies'. Sometimes they gave us tiny cones of newspaper into which they had poured some peanuts or, even more delicious, the curry flavoured mixture we knew as Bombay Mix. If they didn't offer we would beg Ayah, not understanding her often impecunious state, to buy some for us. She rarely refused and probably ate a very meagre supper that night because of it. None of this would have had the approval of my mother, and neither would another occasion when I was taken, this time by Kanaan, to witness a funeral procession passing the end of our lane.

My parents were out and, on hearing a tremendous din coming from the end of our road, I asked Kanaan what was going on.

"We go looking, Missie," he said, and led me down to the T-junction just in time to see a funeral bier being carried aloft by a number of men followed by wailing mourners. The body, partially covered by a cloth and flowers, was visible and the crowd were loudly expressing their grief accompanied by a banging of drums.

"This man very important man in village," Kanaan told me.

It was the first time I had seen a dead body and the image would stay with me for days.

"Where will they bury him?" I asked.

"No Missie, not burying but burning," he replied.

I was silent as we walked back up the lane to our house. Then, just before we came to our gate, we came across another body lying quite still in the middle of the road. He was completely naked and I had seen him often from the car as we swerved around his motionless body. Joseph, our driver, would reassure us that he was not dead. Now I asked Kanaan, "Why does he do that?"

"He is mad man," Kanaan replied. "His family keeping him and feeding him, but they cannot watch him all the time. Don't worry, Missie, he not hurting anyone."

"He's not begging?" I enquired. When we went shopping, I was accustomed to armless old men or small boys hurrying after us on their leg stumps, begging for bakshees.

"No, Missie," Kanaan replied in a matter of fact voice. "He's just mad."

It seemed that Indian families unquestioningly looked after their sick and their old. Our Ayah had a very old mother who lived with her in her godown at the back of the compound. Though not demented, she sometimes had loud and raucous arguments with neighbouring servants. She helped Ayah prepare her food and occasionally let me practise winnowing the chaff from the rice. The implement used for this was a large flat basket shaped like a dustpan without the handle and wielded with a rhythmic grace to toss the rice again and again into the air. The angle at which it was re-caught in the basket allowed the heavier rice to fall at the back. The husks, being lighter, fell straight to the floor or the front of the basket, from where they were discarded by a tilt of the hand. I always managed to spill more rice on the ground than unwanted husks. Amma, as Ayah called her mother, just squatted there with her back against the wall and laughed at me. When I found her grinding spices on a stone block, I wanted to try that too, but she would not let me near her heavy stone roller. She was also adept at milking Ayah's troublesome goat.

Whether Amma was a Catholic, or a Hindu who had arranged to have her daughter educated by Catholic nuns, I do not know, but there was no little Hindu shrine to which to do puja in the godown. Instead Ayah kept a picture of the Virgin Mary on the wall, and hung next to it, her rosary.

Because of us, her charges, she did not manage to get to Mass very often, but always told us she had prayed for us and, according to her daughters, did so until she died, long after we had left India.

CHAPTER EIGHT

THE FLOOD

I sat at the top of the steps leading to our front verandah and wished it would rain; it was eight o'clock at night and still so hot and sultry. My parents had gone out for the evening and sitting with me was Kanaan, our bearer. We were waiting for two things; The Madras Mail, a newspaper usually delivered at about that hour and, far more important, for the monsoon to break. The rains had been expected for days and I was tired of being hot and sticky, even under the whirring, creaking fans that we kept going in every room. My father had gone out without his dinner jacket, a concession allowed in this season known as the Hot Weather, provided he wore a black tie and cummerbund. My mother fared much better in her flimsy voile dresses, which were considered suitable evening wear.

The delivery boy arrived and handed over the evening paper. I was always keen to get hold of it before anybody else because I was avidly following the adventures of Curly Wee, the pig in a comic strip, which the Mail published nightly. While I was reading it, Kanaan called for Muthu, the chokra (his assistant), and they began their usual task of rolling up the rugs before closing the doors for the night.

The carpets were my father's pride and joy. He had collected them through his years in the East, and Kanaan was charged with their care. Spilling lemonade or anything sweet on them was a grave misdemeanour. It was explained to us that the ants would soon be there to eat away at the sugar and whatever it adhered to; so if we had any spills we called urgently for Kanaan to come and clean up the mess.

My mother and father, Ena and Cyril, out for the evening

The verandah doors were closed, though not locked so that my parents could get in, and we retired for the night. Not long afterwards the downpour began. There was thunder and lightning and the rain came down in torrents. By morning, we knew that the monsoon had begun. All day long the rain drummed relentlessly on the tin roof of the garage. The frogs in the tank, from which our flower-beds were watered, set up a constant croaking. The water appeared to fall from the sky in sheets. After two days without let-up the servants came with stories that the level of the River Cooum, which was about a quarter-of-a-mile away, was rising and people feared it would flood. This was very worrying because some of our servants lived in a village of mud and thatch huts near its banks.

We realised what had happened when our neighbours, who lived upstairs, told us that the night before they had had to come home in a rickshaw. They had left their car and driver on dry land and, in a long evening dress and tuxedo, had climbed into a hand-pulled rickshaw. Because its wheels were so high off the ground they reckoned they would be able to keep dry getting home, while the poor rickshaw-wallah had to wade through knee-deep water at the end of our lane.

By lunch time, the water was in our garden and lapping at the bottom of the verandah steps. My sisters and I found it all very exciting. It was still raining and there was no knowing how far the waters would rise. My father's first reaction was to get the precious rugs rolled up and placed on tables. Then my mother called Munswami, the waterman, who lived in the village, and he confirmed that many dwellings there were awash. He and his wife had hung as many belongings as possible from the inside of their roof and had brought their children to our compound. When even that went under water, they camped on our back verandah. The other servants, who had living quarters in the compound, were lucky to have the bungalow's flat roof on which to take refuge.

The rain was incessant. My sisters and I watched in fascination as the swirling waters rose, step by step, towards the level of our verandah. The only thing to be seen in the garden, apart from trees and water, was the folly. This was a round, concrete edifice built in tiers, rather like a wedding cake, with a moat around it, and occasionally used to display plants and ferns on its graduated steps. It was no more than 12 feet across at its widest and 6 feet tall at its peak. So it poked above the water.

Then I had what I thought was a brilliant idea.

"Daddy, couldn't I lie on the Lilo and paddle out to the folly?" I ventured. The Lilo was an inflated mattress that everyone slept on.

My father was adamant. "Most certainly not," he said. "Just watch the water. Can't you see the snakes slithering through it? And there are scorpions. You could be bitten or otherwise catch some dreadful disease from that filthy water if you fell in."

Disappointed, I contented myself with playing with the children on the back verandah. A rubber ball floated away when an erratic throw missed its would-be catcher. The skipping rope was enthusiastically turned and, when told to quieten down, we played 'Fives', the game where you throw five stones in the air and try to catch them on the back of your hand.

We'd all wanted the monsoon to break, but now we just wished the endless rain would stop. Gradually it became more intermittent, and finally the water began to subside. Although grateful it hadn't reached over our verandah, from the branches and other debris floating away, we realised that it must have done a lot of damage.

A few days later, when the water had all gone, we were able to walk in the garden and inspect the moat around the folly. The sun had almost dried it out and I was horrified to see the number of dead snakes there, trapped by the concrete and unable to wiggle away. It was just as well that my father had forbidden my crazy plan, and even more fortunate that the servants' children had been able to take refuge on our back verandah.

With my father carrying Jane, I brave the waves at Madras Beach

Madras Beach

One of our holiday pleasures was going to the beach. Madras is alleged to have the second longest urban beach in the world, and it played a significant part in my childhood. The two sections we frequented were known as Elliots Beach and Cathedral Beach. When we were very young we were often taken by our driver, Fatty, together with Ayah, to Cathedral Beach on very hot evenings to catch the sea breezes. Ayah would let us get our feet wet, but insisted that we stay close by her side as she hitched up her pristine white sari and watched for any turbulent waves. At that time of evening, the beach was busy with locals taking the evening air, and with vendors selling peanuts and sweet-meats, as well as coconuts slashed to enable people to drink the refreshing milk. As we left the beach, there were taps near the pavement where we could wash the sand off our feet before climbing back into the car and travelling home with our heads stuck out of the sliding open roof. Had our parents been with us, this would not have been allowed, but our rotund and jolly driver was always prepared to humour his little Missies.

Elliot's Beach was a little further from the centre of town and much more rustic. Casuarina trees and coconut palms grew down to the edge of the beach and, amongst them, the local fishermen had built their huts of woven palm fronds. They had also built a few huts right at the edge of the sands which, for a few annas (former monetary unit), they rented to bathers as beach huts for changing out of wet swimsuits. Some of these huts had an awning of woven palm leaves in front of them, which was useful if you wanted to go to the beach for the day and eat your picnic in the shade.

The fishermen had two types of vessel for their fishing. The larger, in which they went farther out to sea, was about 10 feet long and 4 feet wide at the top and tapered to their keel about 4 feet down. They were often drawn up on the beach, and we children loved to clamber inside them. It was quite a feat to get in and out, and we sometimes had to enlist an adult's help to pull us out.

For fishing nearer to the shore, the fishermen used a type of catamaran; two or three well-seasoned logs held together by rope on which they could surf to shore at tremendous speed on the quite turbulent waves. This was a thrill we occasionally enjoyed if we could persuade our parents to pay the small fee for which a fisherman would take you a little way out and bring you in on the crest of a wave. As we were all strong swimmers, we did not worry about falling off the catamaran, but so skilled were the fishermen at judging the waves, that they never deposited us into the sea. The only time I was tumbled over and over, grazing my arms and legs in the process, was when I tried, with no surfboard, to coast in on a particularly gigantic wave. It was an unpleasant experience I never repeated.

Mostly the swimming was safe, but just occasionally the fishermen would warn us that there were sharks about. One day we were on Elliot's Beach digging for tiny crabs in the sand at the water's edge, when we heard a lot of shouting.

"Something is happening out there," I said to my sister

Jane, pointing to a fisherman on a catamaran out at sea.

We watched as he hauled a small boy out of the water and then manoeuvred with his pole to catch the next wave to bring them to shore. By this time, a small crowd had collected and immediately surrounded the two when they reached the beach. They were all jabbering in Tamil and we asked Fatty, who had gone to see what the commotion was about, what had happened. The boy had accompanied his father to fish and had dived into the water. Seconds later, the fisherman had spotted a shark a couple of yards away, shouted to his son and was able to drag him up to safety. The boy looked shaken and a woman, probably his mother, was still haranguing the fisherman, no doubt upbraiding him for putting her son in danger. After that, we didn't go to the beach for a couple of weeks.

Further off the Madras coast, there were more sharks and some people went shark fishing. When I was fourteen, I was invited to go on a boat out of Madras harbour to watch them being caught.

"I'm not going," said Jane. "The boat will rock and I'll only be sick." She always preferred to be in the sea rather than on it.

"I won't be," I said with certainty, and accepted the invitation with excitement.

We set out on a lovely sunny morning. I was the only child on board, and it was explained to me that the fisher-men would throw chunks of raw meat overboard to lure the sharks. Once outside the harbour, the boat did begin to rock a little and I leaned over the side, watching intently because I had never seen a shark before. The further we got from the shore, the more the little boat wallowed up and down between waves. As I crossed to the other side of the deck, hoping for a sighting, I began to feel queasy. My discomfort was not helped by the sight of raw red meat piled ready for discharge overboard. The boat gave another great lurch and I knew that I was going to throw up. I clung tightly to the rail and closed my eyes, trying hard not to bring up my breakfast.

But it was no good. I was violently sick over the side and covered with shame, if not with vomit. A kind 'Aunt' led me below deck and made me lie down on a bunk. I stayed there until we got back to still harbour waters. I had not sighted a single shark, let alone seen one being caught.

"I told you," said Jane on my return home.

Elliot's Beach nearly came to play a much more sinister role in our lives. In 1942, after the Japanese had taken Singapore, there was great trepidation that they would cross the Bay of Bengal and land on India's Coromandel Coast. It was thought that a likely target would be the city of Madras, where we had little or no army to defend us. When the situation began to look really serious and rumours spread that the Japanese would be coming ashore at Elliot's Beach, a group of European civilian men decided to patrol it at night. The only weapons they had were their shotguns, which they used for shooting snipe, a popular weekend pastime.

It was years later that my father told me the story of how he and about thirty of his contemporaries had spread out on the beach and walked back and forth along it, their eyes glued to the dark sea and the crashing waves, for several nights. After the first night, an eccentric old burra-sahib had decided to take along his bearer, together with an ice box, to serve him a whiskey-soda after each circuit. My father made the whole thing sound like a complete farce, a Dad's Army in India. But there is no doubt that everyone was scared. Having heard what happened to the Europeans at Changi after the Japanese took Singapore, I remain grateful that the beach in Madras played only a benign role in my life.

POOLSIDE PLAYERS

Jane in action from the Gymkhana Club diving boards

During the school holidays we often went swimming. The Madras Gymkhana Club had a large pool with a slide and numerous diving boards, the highest of which was 20 feet. Few of us school children dared to jump off this, let alone dive from it, but we made good use of the lower boards, particularly for games of 'Follow the Leader'. For this, we vied with each other to think up new and unusual ways by which to enter the pool and that were difficult to copy. If imagination failed, there was always the belly flop or the honey pot, where you jumped in with arms clasped around bent up knees. Both of these displaced large amounts of water and were not appreciated by adults sun-bathing at the side of the pool. Running around the pool, most of us got extremely sunburnt, as sunblock with any factor of protection did not yet exist. To mitigate the effects, we were anointed with calamine lotion when we got home.

To one side of the pool, there was a shady covered terrace where the mothers sat with cool drinks and gossiped while ostensibly keeping an eye on our antics. There was a pool man who raked the water for leaves, and numerous young pool boys dressed in white shirts and shorts with little red fezzes, who brought the nimbu panis (lime juice with water or soda) and any snacks that we ordered. My favourites were a large slice of chocolate cake, or chips with tomato ketchup. When we came with other children and my mother was not there, I was allowed to sign the chits (bills) for refreshments, which went on each member's monthly account. The pool boys had to be extremely careful when bringing our food and constantly watched the skies because kites would hover and make a sudden swoop to snatch a tasty chip or two. They usually shielded the plates with an empty tray, and warned us to look out for the big vicious birds.

Another person who looked after our welfare was the Ladies Room ayah. She rinsed out our bathing costumes and used a hairdryer to dry our hair, as well as producing towels when required. She was on duty all day long and sometimes long into the night, when there was a Club dance. She handed out safety pins and cotton wool when needed, and must have watched over many a tipsy memsahib who retreated to the Ladies Room chaise longue to recover. We girls certainly thought of her as a friend, and particularly so when we played a game with visiting schoolboys to capture the rubber discs we dived for in the pool.

These black discs were round and heavy and sank quickly to the bottom of the pool. Our aim was to keep as many as possible out of the possession of the boys, many of whom were flown out from Britain for the holidays by their parents' Companies. We were all adept at swimming under water but needed to hold our breath for a long time to gather the discs from the deep end. At the end of the morning we would take our stash to the Ladies Room ayah to hide for us, so that we could start the next morning with an advantage. I sometimes suspected that she colluded with the attendant in the Men's changing room and that the discs were divided between them to even up the game.

The children who were flown out to India every holiday were the lucky ones. Some Companies paid for only one holiday a year and others did not pay at all. Few parents could afford to pay for their children to fly half way across the world at the end of every term, which meant long separations, but nothing like those endured in the years before air travel became commonplace. I was thankful that my parents had decided, after five years of leaving us at school in England, to send us to a boarding school in an Indian hill station, Ootacamund (now Udagamandalam).

We enjoyed the company of our new playmates and must have made a noisy, boisterous crowd at the swimming pool, running around and splashing in and out of it. During a holiday, probably to curb our unruly behaviour, one of the mothers decided to get us girls to perform a water ballet. Many of us were fans of the swimming film star, Esther Williams, so we embraced her idea with enthusiasm. We were made to swim in unison, to practise graceful somersaults and a host of other manoeuvres, including floating in formation with one leg extended into the air at right angles to our body. The latter exercise resulted in much giggling and many submersions, but we eventually got the hang of it and became a fairly synchronised team.

Meantime, the boys were practising diving, because the Club held an annual Swimming Gala, which included a diving competition. One or two became expert divers, good enough to beat any adult. It was suggested that, at the Gala, we should give a performance of our water ballet to club members, but we decided that we needed weeks and weeks more practice, by which time half our number would have flown back to school in Britain. So we promised to get together next holidays to continue our rehearsals.

On the last holiday morning, I ordered chips and

ketchup for a group of us.

"I'm hungry," said my little sister Sue, and as soon as she saw the pool boy approaching with the tray of food, she ran out from under the roofed terrace and took a plate of chips.

"Be careful, Missie," the pool boy warned her, but not in time. As she picked up a chip, there was a sudden swoosh. A large kite dropped out of the sky and attacked her plate, but it was not chips his vicious beak met with, it was her fingers. Sue gave a shriek and dropped the plate, scattering chips everywhere. She ran to my mother, her finger torn and bloody. A second pool boy scurried to pick up the food because more kites had spotted the scattered remains and were gathering overhead.

We took Sue up to the Ladies Room to wash her wounds with fresh water. The ayah produced plasters and iodine to disinfect the blood-covered finger. My little sister had had quite a shock, and never again did we eat our poolside snacks in the open, but remained under the covered terrace until every last bit had been consumed.

THE SWIMMING GALA

As the Swimming Gala approached, excitement grew amongst the children who frequented the pool at the Gym (Gymkhana Club). The Gala was held in the Cold Weather and our numbers were augmented by several boys and girls who had been flown from Britain to spend the Christmas holidays with their parents. Although there were special races for the under tens, anybody older could participate in the adult races, and we were keen to pit our abilities against the grown ups. We trained endlessly, and mothers who normally spent their mornings gossiping in the shade of the cool verandah, were roped in to time lengths completed by breast stroke, back stroke, crawl and any other variation we could come up with. They were solicited to pronounce on the performance of dives from the springboard, the 20 foot board and every board between. We certainly hoped that one of the boys, a particularly proficient diver, would carry off the prize in the adult diving competition.

Then there was the water ballet, which we girls were to perform. After weeks of practise, we had been considered good enough to be billed as one of the highlights of the Gala agenda. As one could not buy swimsuits in India at that time, there was no question of our synchronising our outfits, but Olga, our coach, had drilled us to synchronise our movements until we came out of the pool with goose pimples after every session. We were, nevertheless, a little nervous.

On the much anticipated Sunday morning, my parents, sisters Jane and Sue and I arrived to find many friends gathered around the pool. The young chokras (pool boys) in their scarlet fezzes were busy serving cold drinks and, to those hung over from the Gym's Saturday night dance, stronger pick-me-ups. We ran upstairs to change. The Ladies Room ayah had her hands full with little girls pulling on their bathing costumes all around her, and more sedate memsahibs trying to protect their modesty behind cubicle curtains.

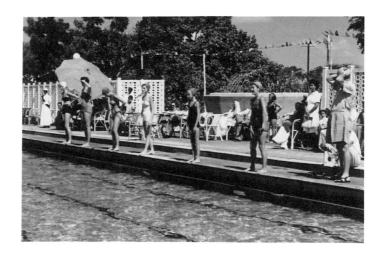

The Swimming Gala.
From right: Olga, Jane, myself, Ann Livy, Joan, Janice

When we arrived back at the pool, our parents had found themselves a table under an umbrella near the shallow end. The man we called 'Uncle Alan' was announcing the first race through a loud hailer.

"The Men's Freestyle race will be swum over two lengths," he propounded, "and I hope to see some of you older boys taking part in it."

We knew our friend, Mike, was going to try for it and we gave him the thumbs-up sign as he walked past our table. There was a great splash as the contestants hit the water in a racing dive, and we searched for Mike's blonde head, which came up third from the front. After the turn, he was second and we jumped up and down with excitement as he ploughed closer to the leading swimmer. But the older man, with a burst of speed, pulled away to finish a yard in front of our friend.

The third race was for children under the age of six. Sue was to take part in this, and was expected to swim only the width of the pool. Her older sisters gave her plenty of advice.

"Uncle' Alan will shout, 'Are you ready, get set, go', and you must not let go of the side of the pool until he says GO," I instructed her.

She nodded, and with a look of determination on her face, climbed into the water. We had been trying to teach her the breast stroke, but with four little girls and three boys, she dog paddled her way across the pool to reach the finish just ahead of her nearest rival. We were delighted, even though it had not been a display of conventional swimming strokes.

"That deserves an ice cream," my father told her, as my mother towelled her dry.

Neither Jane nor I were as successful as our little sister in the races we took part in. We were waiting nervously for our appearance in the water ballet, which was to be the finale of the Gala. Still to come, however, was the diving competition. We had high hopes for our friend, Harry, a sixteen-year old who was out from England to spend Christmas with his parents. He told us he had a very good diving coach at his school and it certainly showed when he took to the boards. He even tried to improve some of our performances by passing on his expertise. But none of the rest of us felt good enough to enter a competition, which was open to all the adults who swam and dived regularly at the Gym.

The contestants started off with dives from the lower springboard. Harry's jack knife was perfect. They proceeded to the next levels, eight divers in all, giving varied performances from each board. Harry managed faultless dives, including a graceful swallow dive from the 15 foot board. They came to the top 20 foot board, and it was announced that from here they must include a somersault. On occasions we had watched Harry muff this dive, and we waited with bated breath as he came to the edge of the board. Seconds later, it was all over. He had executed a perfect somersault and entered the pool at an absolute right angle to its surface. Nobody else had managed such an elegant dive, and Harry was duly declared winner of the competition and loudly applauded.

Including my sister Jane, there were eight of us taking part in the water ballet, all girls between the ages of eleven and fifteen. We were enthusiastic swimmers, though not as graceful as warranted by a ballet. But we all aspired to be miniature Esther Williams's, whose films we always went to see when they were shown at Madras cinemas.

Now, in our assorted swimsuits, we took our places in the pool. At the drop of Olga's hand we started our routine, swimming in circles, forming stars and performing underwater somersaults and handstands. Our arms and legs waved, we hoped gracefully, in the air. To our relief, nobody made a mistake, and our finale was greeted with much applause.

This was followed by the prize giving. Several silver-plated cups were awarded, and sister Sue received one as 'Winner - Under Six Freestyle'. Then came a surprise.

"We would like to thank Olga and her girls for their splendid performance," said 'Uncle' Alan, "and the Committee has decided to give the team matching swim-suits. These will be bought in Singapore by a Member who is soon going there on holiday, so will each girl please give Olga her size by next Sunday. Olga has chosen the colour scarlet for her 'Madras Mermaids'."

THEATRICALS

Jane and I request autographs at Gemini Film Studios in Madras

The film industry in Madras, though not on the scale of the Bollywood film productions in Bombay, was mainly repre-sented by a large complex known as Gemini Studios. One day, Jane and I were asked if we would like to accompany an 'Aunt' who had been invited to tour the Studios. We accepted with alacrity as we were fanatic film fans, though we knew nothing about Indian films.

On arrival, we were all garlanded and offered tea. Then we toured the sets, which were enormous and extremely colourful. I could now understand why the advertising hoardings which beamed down on us all over Madras were so vivid. We were introduced to two of the stars, attired for their parts in a film that was being made, and watched a take. Before leaving, I asked for the name of the next film that would appear on general release in Madras cinemas. When we eventually went to see it, I was somewhat disappointed. Perhaps it was because the sound track in the cinema was so loud, but mainly because I had to try and follow the story by sight alone, as the little Tamil I knew was of no help at all. We also did not understand why the scene always faded just as the hero was about to kiss the heroine.

Jane and I decided to stick to films in English and went often, mainly to Hollywood musicals and particularly those starring Fred Astaire and Ginger Rogers. Jane's best friend, our doctor's daughter who lived next door, often accompanied us. After watching, Noreen was adept at making up dance routines, and she and Jane would dress up and give performances to amuse our parents. We had a tin trunk that contained our dressing-up clothes. In it were shawls, old hats, jockeys' silks and components of the fancy dress costumes, which my parents had to invent afresh for every New Year's Eve dance.

There was no sari in our dressing-up box but I wanted to know how to put one on, so I asked Ayah. She normally wore dazzlingly white saris almost as a uniform, but she brought one of her coloured ones and with it a petticoat with a drawstring waist. The latter she insisted, was a necessity, as one needed to tuck in and anchor the pleats one folded into the front of the sari before pulling it round and over the shoulder. Ayah never wore flowers in her hair, but many women, even the poorer ones, did. In the bazaar, we watched vendors sitting amidst a mass of blooms, patiently threading jasmine and marigolds onto strings, which became hair ornaments and garlands to be offered on special occasions.

Some garlands were made with silver and gold thread and were much more expensive. Of these, we had saved a couple for our dressing up trunk after they had been placed around my father's neck by his insurance agents, who always came to pay their respects on New Year's morning. They often came with baskets of fruit and would stay and talk for a few minutes, while my father was probably nursing a headache from the party the night before.

In Madras, New Year's Eve was always celebrated by the Europeans and wealthier Indians with a big fancy dress party. People, in their various guises, would gather for dinner parties at homes around the city, and then go on to a dance held at the Adyar Club or the Gymkhana Club. At midnight, everybody on the dance floor formed a huge circle and sang 'Auld Lang Syne'. Some would go from one club to the other and continue celebrating well into the next morning. The year I was fifteen, I was dressed as a gypsy and allowed to go to the dinner at 'Auntie' Bess's house but not to the Club's dance to see in the New Year. For that I had to wait until I was seventeen.

'Auntie' Bess was my mother's best friend whose son Patrick was one of my playmates until he was sent away to boarding school in England. I think 'Auntie' Bess missed not having a daughter and, in later years, she invited me round some afternoons and kept me amused by showing me how to do things like covering a box with material and making a lampshade. I've had an interest in craft work ever since.

One year, she and some of our other 'Aunts' organised an evening for charity. Stalls were set up in a big garden, and guests could fish for floating plastic ducks or have a go at rifle shooting to win a prize. I had never been allowed near my father's prized shotgun, but that evening he showed me how to hold a rifle and aim for the bullseye. The kickback almost knocked me over, and I decided that shooting would never be a sport for me. There was food and dancing, and entertainment in which I took a small part. Dressed all in green, as an Irish colleen, I had to take to the stage alone and dance an Irish jig. I was more than a little nervous, but comforted by the thought that the audience consisted mostly of forgiving 'Aunts' and 'Uncles' — unlike poor Jane who had had to dance as Puck some weeks earlier before a hundred or so strangers at a Government House reception. She was petrified, but our dancing mistress had been so proud that one of her pupils had been asked to perform at such an august venue, that Jane felt she had to do it. In spite of her nerves, she danced

Jane dances as 'Puck' at Government House, Madras

beautifully and received tumultuous applause.

After my performance, I played a less nerve-racking role for the rest of the evening. Wearing a short skater skirt and jaunty pillbox, and with a tray slung from my neck, I had to try and persuade people to buy cigarettes which had been donated for the charity. Everybody was very generous and seemed to enjoy the occasion. It made a change from the more usual round of cocktail and dinner parties in each other's homes and dances at the Clubs. Occasionally a band of actors arrived from England and staged a play, and from time to time enthusiastic members of an amateur dramatic group put on a production. But mainly, we relied on the cinema for our entertainment, and my childhood pin-ups were the Hollywood film stars of the day.

CHAPTER NINE

GOING 'HOME' ON LEAVE

When my parents were due to go on home leave in April 1952, they decided to take their three children with them. This meant that we would be out of our school in Ootacamund for six months. We were going to stay with my grandmother in Bedford, and they reckoned they could get Jane and me into the High School there for the summer and part of the autumn term.

We sailed from Bombay in the S.S. Strathmore, which came from Australia. The P&O ships that called at Bombay had two runs, either to and from Hong Kong or Australia. This made for very differing passenger lists, with the ships coming from Sydney being full of young Australians on their first visit to England. As a fifteen-year old this suited me just fine because, although I was too young to join in their camaraderie, I still appreciated the girls' snazzy clothes, the young men's tans, and the invitations to join them at deck tennis and deck quoits.

I was old enough to take my meals with the adults, whereas Jane who was not quite twelve, was relegated to children's mealtimes with Sue. Although I had no long dresses, I still felt very grown up changing for dinner, and was always ready when the small page-boy in his red jacket toured the decks loudly banging his gong, which he did to announce each mealtime. The menus were beautifully produced, with an illustration on the cover. The theme of this voyage was 'Cries of London' and we had reproductions of water colour paintings depicting flower sellers, barrow boys and others, which I collected throughout our journey. I was allowed my first taste of wine on this trip, and my father ordered a bottle of German wine because he thought I would like the sweetness of it. But mostly the colonials drank long whiskey-sodas, while the young Australians consumed large quantities of beer, especially gathered around the swimming pool before lunch.

I was allowed to stay up and take part in the evening's entertainment. Some nights there was bingo and on other nights, horse racing. For the latter, passengers volunteered to be jockeys, which entailed pulling a wooden horse along the deck or race course, without letting it fall over. There was betting, which I never did, but I volunteered as a jockey.

The evenings I enjoyed most were when there was dancing. As soon as the ship's band struck up, I would beg my father, "Please Dad, dance with me." Sometimes the ship's officers took pity on him and asked me to dance. They were so handsome in their dress uniforms and I was thrilled. I felt sorry that Jane could not take part in the dancing. She too would have plagued my father to dance with her. During the day we were inseparable and roamed all over the ship, running round the decks and splashing in the pool, which was not very large but enabled us to cool off early in the voyage. When darkness fell we'd lean over the railings, trying to make out whether lights in the distance were other ships or just stars, and listen to the waves lapping against the hull.

When the Strathmore anchored off shore at Aden in what is now called Yemen, we were hanging over the railings again to watch the small boys who dived for coins, which the passengers threw out to them. I think Aden must have been a duty free port, because many people came back from trips ashore with cameras, radios and watches.

Then we came to Suez and the Canal.

"I can't believe we can sail so close to the land without running aground," said Jane, as we steamed slowly through. Half-way along, other ships were waiting in the Pool for their turn to pass through in the opposite direction. There was a lot of waving and shouting and sounding of ships' horns as we acknowledged one another. Finally we arrived at Port Said. Before long, we heard the raucous shouts of vendors below.

"Come and look, come and look," Jane called. "They've got all sorts of things in their boats."

I left little Sue, who was watching the Gully Gully Man as he produced fluffy baby chicks from children's eyes, noses and armpits. I leaned over the railings as far as I could to see that a small flotilla of rowing boats had attached themselves like barnacles to the side of our huge white liner.

"That one is going to get the overflow pipe all over him if he's not careful," said Jane.

"What are they shouting, can you hear?" I asked her.

"No, but I think he wants us to buy one of those bags with patterns all over it. And he's got a pouffe."

"I'll have one of those," said Mr. Billingshurst, a passenger who had come up beside us. He shouted and gestured at one of the men below, who immediately took aim at him with a piece of rope. Mr. Billingshurst was not quick enough. It fell back into the rowing boat and was only caught on the third attempt. We watched, fascinated. The man below tied a basket to his end of the rope and sent up a pouffe for Mr. Billingshurst's inspection.

"Can we look, please," we asked.

"Alright," said Mr. Billingshurst, feeling in his pocket for his wallet. "He wants a lot of money for it, and I think I'll offer him a third."

He leaned over and shouted down. There was a sharp tug on the rope as the vendor shook his head in an emphatic "No." The haggling went on as we held firmly to our end of the rope.

"Do you really want it?" I asked Mr. Billingshurst.

"I think it would make a nice present for my Aunt Edith," he said, and finally settled for just over half the price originally quoted.

Then it was time to go ashore with our parents. From the end of the gangway, we walked across the pontoons in single file with my father leading the way.

"You want guide? You want guide?" we were asked by innumerable men in red fezzes and white djellabas, who were greeting the passengers from the S.S. Strathmore. We were bound for Simon Artz, Port Said's one big store, to which my father had found his way many times before, so we declined all offers. It was a relief to get out of the heat into the shop's cool white interior. We toured the galleried floors, from which one could look down into the central well, and were thankful for the whirring fans and our escape from the tumult outside.

There was no changing to evening dress that evening, as the ship sailed out into the Mediterranean. We were leaving the East behind and, as my mother put it:

"We're now really on our way home."

As the weather became cooler we needed our warmer clothes, and this entailed visits to the Baggage Room. Apart from the trunks that went into the hold, and were therefore labelled 'Not Wanted on Voyage', our luggage was divided into suitcases that came into the cabin and those 'Wanted on Voyage', which went into the Baggage Room. This was only open at specific times, and going there was an unpacking and packing ritual we all needed to undertake.

While the Mediterranean was calm and balmy, the Bay of Biscay was a different matter. It was known for its turbulence and on this voyage, it lived up to its reputation. As the ship rolled and wallowed, crockery slid across the tables and we staggered from side to side of the corridors when trying to reach our cabins. In them many passengers remained, unable to face any meals if not actually vomiting. One of those afflicted was Jane. She took to her bunk and lay there curled up in misery with a basin on the floor beside her. The next morning I cajoled:

"Come up on deck. The fresh air will make you feel better."

"No it won't," she muttered, and turned to face the wall.

"Dad is playing in the final of the deck tennis competition this morning," I informed her. "Don't you want to come and cheer him on?"

"I can't," she moaned. "Anyway, they won't play while we're rolling like this."

I gave up and went away. I was lucky to have good sea legs.

The weather improved, and we steamed up the English Channel on a bright, sunny morning, our eyes skinned for a first sighting of the white cliffs of Dover. Our port of disembarkation was Tilbury, but after years away, it was the white cliffs of Dover that confirmed for every Englishman that he was finally 'home'.

ENGLAND REVISITED

After two and a half years away, our return to Bedford was greeted with delight and much hugging and kissing by our grandparents. We awaited eagerly the weekend visit of Aunt Mary and cousin Brian, who was now a boarder at St. Paul's School in London. Soon it would be our turn to go back to school. After a couple of weeks, Jane and I entered, somewhat hesitantly, the forbidding enormity of Bedford High School. Jane had never been there before and was put in a class of girls of her age. I returned to sit amongst the classmates I had left behind in 1949. My former friends were still there, and I was relieved to find that my education had obviously not suffered; the only subject I had some difficulty with was Science.

Gymnastics and Games were considered an important part of the School's curriculum, and I was grateful for the afternoons I had spent returning balls aimed at me by the

Tennis Marker at the Madras Cricket Club. Although I had been watching my father play cricket from the time I could sit up in a pram, I had never actually taken part in a game myself. In summer, at the High School, we were coached by girls from the Bedford Physical Training College, who taught us to bat and bowl, as well as the names of all the fielding positions. The one I will never forget is 'Silly Mid-On' where, one afternoon, I took a hard hit ball on the left eye and appeared for weeks afterwards with a black, purple, green and then yellow eye-socket. The 'Silly' part of this position has always struck me as very appropriate.

Although there were some Houses for boarders, the majority of girls at the school were day pupils. Those who lived in our part of town belonged to St. John House, and our summer uniform was blue and white gingham dresses. These my mother bought us as she thought we could even wear them in India. For the short period of the autumn term that we would attend the High School, it was agreed that we could wear our own clothes rather than kitting us out in the heavy navy items, which were the regulation uniform. Thus dressed, I felt somewhat out of place in those latter weeks, but knew that we would soon be having another glorious holiday, both on board ship and back in Madras for the Cold Weather.

In England, we enjoyed the school summer holidays. As early birthday presents, Jane and I had each been given splendid red bicycles with semi-dropped handlebars, which we considered very cool. We used them to ride to school, but even more when term ended and we could explore the countryside which was on Grandma's doorstep. One of the villages we visited by car was Biggleswade, where my parents had friends with a farm. There the family held tennis parties and took us swimming in the river nearby. Being used to a chlorinated pool warmed by a tropical sun, it was strange to feel plants brushing your legs as you waded into the cool dark water.

When I was younger I did not appreciate what a pleasant town Bedford was. I thought of it only as the place that kept me away from my parents and away from India. Now at fifteen, and without the prospect of being marooned there, I began to see it in a different light. I had always enjoyed the swimming pool at the end of our road, which was formed with the river running through it, and now I saw other agreeable aspects of the River Great Ouse. It had a tree-lined embankment along which you could cycle all the way up to the main part of town. The river was frequented by swans and rowers from the two big boys' schools, so there was always something to watch. On the other side of the Embankment road was a park with a playground, where Jane and I took Sue to play on the swings and surreptitiously used them ourselves. We cycled without fear through the centre of town to school, and were reminded every morning, by his statue which we passed, that John Bunyan was born in the village of Elstow just outside Bedford, and The Pilgrims' Progress was required reading. There was another big park, Russell Park, near Bedford School and there, with friends and our bikes, I sometimes loitered, chatting to pupils they knew.

On the High Street, there was a large department store where we bought clothes and shoes, though there was one shop that did nothing but supply the uniforms for all the schools in town. Most fun to visit was the Saturday market in front of the Corn Exchange, to which farmers from surrounding areas brought their produce. Apart from the usual fruit and vegetables, we occasionally found a stall selling bananas, which were something Jane and I missed. Afterwards, our parents took us to the nearby Swan Hotel for coffee and ice cream. The hotel overlooked the river and was a congenial meeting place for many of their friends, so they sometimes sent us home on our own while they stayed on to have a beer.

During the summer, Bedford School, of which my father was an alumnus, held Old Bedfordians Week. It was another opportunity for my parents to meet up with old friends, and also afforded us entertainment. There were rowing races on the Great Ouse to watch, tennis matches and a cricket match in which my father played for the Old Boys against the school team. My mother, Jane, Sue and I were there, watching with pride and hoping, in vain, that he would score a century.

In the school holidays, we were taken to the ballet in London, and accompanied my mother there on shopping trips for clothes. With nothing comparable in Madras, the big stores like Harrods and Selfridges impressed us greatly. We loved riding the escalators and being sprayed with perfume in the Beauty Departments. Sometimes, we visited Harrods' Banking Hall, now long gone, where we were amused by the old gentlemen resting, and occasionally snoring, in the vast leather armchairs there. Upstairs, my mother would try on evening dresses and ask our opinion.

It was expected in India that women returning from 'home' leave would bring back ready-made dresses to flaunt. These were considered superior to anything you could have run up by your derzi (tailor) despite the fabulous materials available in India. We did notice though that both my grandmother and Aunt Mary seemed to appreciate the undies with beautiful hand embroidery that we had brought them as presents.

One day my mother said to me, "I'm going to take you to Raymond's to have your hair razor cut. It's supposed to make it more curly."

I gathered that Raymond was a renowned London hairdresser, known as Mr. Teasy-Weasy, who had developed a special method of cutting hair that encouraged it to curl. When we arrived at his Knightsbridge salon, it was certainly impressive, with gilt mirrors, chandeliers and assistants and shampoo girls buzzing around everywhere. This was a far cry from Mrs Rajan's, our hairdresser in Madras, who had neither an assistant nor a telephone. In order to get an appointment, we had to send round our waterman, Munswami, with a chit (note), who would then wait and bring back a written reply. I had an appointment with Raymond himself, who duly razor cut my hair, complimented my mother on its condition, and sent us away on payment of a hefty bill. Weeks later, I was still waiting for my straight brown hair to be transformed into curls.

My parents, being horse racing enthusiasts, went to many of the important meetings of the flat racing season when they were on 'home' leave. They planned to go to the July Meeting at Newmarket, and to keep expenses down, they decided to hire a Dormobile and use it as their hotel for the week. Before leaving, they parked it outside Grandma's house, where Jane, Sue and I were able to climb inside and investigate all its features. We begged to be allowed to sleep the night in it, and Jane and I were given permission on the understanding that we kept the door locked and did not open it to anyone except our parents. It was a slightly scary but memorable experience, which we were to recall many years later when my father actually bought a Dormobile. He had retired from the insurance company and, after living restlessly in Kent for a year, decided to travel overland back to India.

My mother could not countenance such a trip, so he took his shotgun and set off in the Dormobile alone. Along the way, he picked up hitchhikers from time to time and eventually, after travelling through Europe, including Yugoslavia and Bulgaria, then Turkey, Iran, Pakistan and India for months, he arrived back in Madras. We then heard he had bought a stud farm in Bangalore and intended to take up a second career as a race horse breeder. My mother joined him, travelling far more conventionally by P&O liner.

As a child of the Raj himself, my father always had a special empathy with the vast sub-continent of India. His mother had brought him and his two brothers and sister 'home' to Bedford School when he was twelve. After joining an insurance company in 1926, he was sent a year later to their Karachi office. Following spells in Lahore, Bombay and Malaysia, he finished as burra-sahib of the

Madras branch. Although he much enjoyed his home leaves, he was always pleased to go back East, just as I now looked forward to returning to India.

CHAPTER TEN

THE RACING TIPSTERS

"Now, eat this spoonful for Old Fogey," cajoled Ayah.

My little sister Sue was baulking, as usual, at eating her spinach, and Ayah had her own ways of getting her to finish her supper.

There was no question that ours was a racing household and even Ayah, who unlike our other servants, was no gambler, knew the names of her employers' race horses.

"This one is for William Bell," she intoned, pushing another mouthful down a reluctant three-year old.

"I don't like spinach," remonstrated Sue, trying to get up from the nursery table.

"Cookie has made it especially for you," Jane told her.

"I'll call him if you like," I added, trying to be helpful.

Jane and I were too old for nursery supper, but had long ago digested Ayah's admonition that 'spinach is good for you'.

"Yes," said Jane, "and then we can tell him what we want to eat tomorrow, before he does the cook's book with Mummy."

'Doing the cook's book' was a daily ritual. Every evening, Cookie took in to my mother his little notebook in which he had written, together with prices, all he had bought that day. My mother would check his figures and then advance him a further amount for the next day's shopping. They would then discuss and decide on the menu. I had looked at the cook's book and had been intrigued by an item noted as 'Bicycle – 8 annas' (former Indian coin). I learned, on questioning, that this was a perk enjoyed by Cookie, and that the 8 annas per day was for wear and tear on his bicycle, which he used to carry back produce from the market. I fetched him now from the kitchen. He was short and plump, probably from tasting too many of the sweet things my father loved to eat. His white shirt, slightly besmirched, hung outside his long white lungi, and his teeth seemed to sparkle in his dark face as he grinned at us. He had been with us almost as long as Kanaan, our bearer, and that was from the time Jane was born.

"Tell Mummy you'll make fish and mango curry for lunch tomorrow Cookie," Jane ordered.

"But Missie, mangos not in season."

"Alright then, fish curry with ladies fingers," I countermanded.

"And chocolate bomb for pudding," added little Sue.

"Very good, Missies, I'm asking Madam," he said, pretending to take us as seriously as he would any burra-memsahib.

"And Cookie, please bring us some very big carrots from the bazaar, because tomorrow we're going to 'Stables'."

"Right Jane Missie, I'm bringing carrots and you telling me what is winning on Sunday."

Late Saturday afternoon in the racing season, my parents always went to 'Stables'. As owners and ardent race goers, this was a ritual they never missed. Stables was the premises of their trainer, Sam, and most of Sam's owners were to be found there of a Saturday evening, sitting in a row of wicker chairs, discussing the next day's prospects, and watching their horses being paraded and then fed.

We children loved to watch as each syce (stable lad) brought out his horse's trough and placed it in a circle. Overseeing the operation was Sam's wife, Sheila, a diminutive woman with the manner of a sergeant-major when ordering the welfare of her horses. Her major-domo or head stable lad was a tall, lanky Pathan, twice her height, with a long curly moustache, and clothed in the baggy trousers and distinctive turban of his tribe. His warrior ancestry was no match for the fiery commands of his employer. Throughout he remained dignified and supportive, repeating Sheila's orders as she shouted at her syces and made sure each horse received the exact amount of oats and whatever other feed she prescribed for them. At a given command, the syces turned on their heels and carried their troughs to their charges, who had already been led back into their stables. Sometimes Mum and Dad would go and stroke the noses of Old Fogey or William Bell or another of their own horses, and would show us how to feed them carrots, always in the flat of our hands to avoid having our fingers munched.

Meantime, Sam was chatting to his owners, all of whom wanted to know which of his runners he fancied for tomorrow. As dusk began to fall, he'd called out 'Boy', and from the house his bearer came running with the whiskey and tray of glasses. Behind him scurried the chokra (boy assistant) bearing the soda water with which most people topped up their glasses to make the long drink favoured by so many British in the colonies. In southern India, darkness falls quickly and, within half-an-hour, the warm velvet black around us was illuminated by innumerable kerosene lamps, some to light the party and others being carried hither and thither by syces finally putting their charges to bed. The crickets had set up their cacophony and winged insects clustered around the lamps, drawn by the pools of light. The mosquitos too came out in force now, and some of the ladies took out pillow cases from their handbags and pulled them up over their bare calves.

A few jockeys, who came to ride in India at the end of the British flat-racing season, dropped by. The conversation was of nothing but horses and racing, and we children listened hard, trying to pick up all the tips to pass on to our servants. Of course, they always asked 'Madam' too before she set off for the race-course, but my mother would only give them a tip if it was as near a 'certainty' as any racing tip can ever be. She knew how many children they all had to feed, and she hated them losing their money and sometimes paid them back their lost stakes.

That evening, Cookie brought Sue her chocolate bomb.

"Especially for you," he told her. "Now Missies, do you know what is winning at the races tomorrow?"

"Uncle Sam says his horse Silver Star has a very good chance," Jane said.

"Yes, I heard him telling someone it was a near certainty," I added.

"Very good, Missies," said Cookie, "I'm putting bet on 'Silver Star' tomorrow morning in the bazaar."

The next day we didn't go to the races with our parents as we sometimes did. 'Uncle' Eric, Patrick's father, was coming to take us children to the beach. He didn't enjoy racing, and while his wife, Bess, went regularly, he often took us swimming with his son. We had a great day and came home tired out by sun, sea and sand. But we didn't want to go to bed and stayed up waiting for our parents to come home.

"Did Silver Star win?" was the first question we asked them.

"No, she ran fourth," replied my mother.

"Oh dear, poor Cookie," said Jane, looking crestfallen.

"Why do you say that?" my mother asked.

"Yesterday, we told him that 'Uncle' Sam thought Silver Star would win today, and he was going to put a bet on her in the bazaar this morning," I told her.

"Oh no," said my mother. "I had better talk to him. Last night, I gave him an advance on his salary because he said his wife needed a special sari for a family wedding."

Cookie was called in and confirmed that he had indeed put all his advance on 'Silver Star'.

"Well," said my mother, "because the Missies gave you that tip, I won't ask you to pay back your advance, but I'm afraid your wife will have to go without her new sari."

Then she turned to us. "You must promise me," she said, very sternly, "that you will never give a racing tip to any of the servants again."

RACING PINK AND CHOCOLATE BROWN

In the Christmas holidays, being taken to the races in Madras was a special treat for us. We felt we were entering an exciting grown up world. People dressed up for the occasion and often wore hats. This was particularly so on New Year's Day, when the crowds in the Members' Enclosure were swelled by non-enthusiasts, who went more for the social occasion. It was at the races one usually heard first that a particular Burra-Sahib had been honoured by the British monarch with a knighthood for services to the business community in India.

"I wish we could have a big win today," said my sister Jane one year, as we followed our parents into the Members' Enclosure. "Then we could buy Christmas presents for Mummy and Daddy out of our own money."

There had been the usual gaggle of small boys at the entrance, all trying to thrust race books into our hands. My father bought us one each. At the races, our parents were always too busy to have much time for us, so they taught us the ropes early on and left us to our own devices. By the time we were eleven and fourteen, Jane and I had learned to risk our pocket money by placing bets on the Tote, to mark up our race cards if jockeys were changed or horses scratched, and to note down the winners.

We mingled with the crowd, amongst whom we found several 'uncles' and 'aunts', and these we accosted for advice on possible winners. They were reluctant to mark our cards but bought us lemonades in the Clubhouse instead. We hung over the paddock railings, smiling at the jockeys we knew, and got a big wink from Shankar, our stable jockey, as he rode past. Even when our parents had a runner, we were not allowed into the paddock, and nor the Bookies' Ring. The latter was between the Members' and Public Enclosures and struck me as such a chaotic place on the one occasion I begged to be taken in, that I never wanted to set foot there again. By comparison, the Members' Enclosure was tranquil. Shaded by huge trees, it was dotted with flowerbeds of Canna lilies, whose brilliant scarlets and oranges vied with the gorgeous hues and shimmering textures of the women's saris.

We'd learned that the best way to make a lot of money was to win a double or a treble.

"Let's try for the double today," I said to Jane, "and not have any other bets. We have to choose in the third and the fifth races."

"One of the horses we pick in the third will have to be our Old Fogey," responded Jane.

"But I heard that 'Uncle' Sam doesn't give him much of a chance," I countered. "He fancies Break Away and has given him to Shankar to ride."

"Then we'll put two tickets on him and two on Old Fogey," was Jane's answer. "We can't leave our horse out."

My father had taught us that to do the double, we should try and have two choices for the second leg. I thought we were wasting our tickets on Old Fogey but sentiment prevailed, and we went up to our box clutching those four tickets.

Our parents had a box high up in the Members' stand, and we knew we would always find them there at the beginning of each race. All the other boxes up there were taken by owners or trainers, so at the end of a race the noise of owners shouting home their horses could be deafening. We waited anxiously for the start of the race and were two of the loudest cheerers when Old Fogey won it by a length. 'Uncle' Sam, his trainer, hurtled down the stairs, precariously followed by my mother in her high heels to lead in her colours of pink and chocolate brown.

"That was a splendid surprise," exclaimed my father, knowing that Sam had expected his other horse, Break Away, to win. We went down to the Clubhouse and celebrated with ice cream.

My mother leads in a winner, in her colours of pink and chocolate brown, together with the trainer, 'Uncle' Sam

We now needed to find the winner of the fifth race. What should we do with our two remaining chances? 'Uncle' Sam did not have a runner in that race. We decided to call in the experts and button-holed Mum and Dad.

"You will have to put one of them on the favourite, High Spirits, and I would put the other on Petra Princess," my father told us.

"Oh I don't know," said my mother. "It's a mile race and I don't think Petra Princess will stay the length. I fancy Coramandel."

"Right girls," said my father. "Go and look at the runners in the paddock. See who looks the healthiest, whether they are playing up or sweating, and then decide between you whether to take Petra Princess or Coramandel for the second ticket."

"I like Coramandel, her colours are so pretty," said Jane.

"Don't be silly, you can't choose by the colours of the jockey's silks," I retorted, "but she is the biggest and the best-groomed."

So we plumped for my mother's recommendation.

When the race started, the favourite hit the front first, closely followed by the purple and gold colours of Petra Princess. Coramandel was in a bunch behind. Our parents had the binoculars, so we could only listen to their commentary until the horses came into the final bend.

"Petra Princess has dropped to fourth, but Coramandel is coming on the outside," announced my mother excitedly. We held our breath and watched as they raced up the straight with Coramandel gaining ground all the time.

"Come on, come on Coramandel," shouted Jane, and the rest of the family joined in lustily.

"She's done it!" I gasped, as Coramandel crossed the line a neck ahead of the favourite. "We've won the double."

And that day, because the favourites had not won, the double paid extremely well.

At Madras Races, from left:
myself, Jane, 'Auntie' Bess, my mother, and 'Auntie' Doris

After the last race, chairs were pulled up around tables under the spreading trees, drinks were ordered, and our celebrating parents joined friends for the usual post-mortem on the day's events. We were packed into the car and sent home with Joseph, our driver, but we didn't mind in the least; we were so delighted with our day's achievement.

We discussed what we would buy as presents.

"We could get Daddy a pewter tankard with Old Fogey engraved on it," I suggested, "to remind him of today. And we could buy Mummy one of those embroidered stoles she was looking at in the Kashmiri shop the other day."

"Yes," said Jane triumphantly, "we could get one in pink and chocolate brown!"

THE END OF THE HOLIDAYS

The time was approaching for six-year old Sue to join us at boarding school. Jane and I had tried to tell her all the good things about it, and her main concern seemed to be that she would be leaving behind 'Chippy'. Chippy was a little grey chipmunk, who had fallen out of the rattan blind as Kanaan was unrolling it. When Sue picked him up, he was tiny and could not have been long born. She made him a nest to sleep in and fed him milk with a dropper. Then, as he grew older, she fed him chopped up pieces of guava, because the many grey chipmunks who lived in our garden seemed to eat all the guavas off our trees. Chippy ran around all over the house and became more and more inquisitive. One day he fell into the lavatory bowl and had to be fished out by Ayah. A week before we were due to leave for school, Sue was feeding him and he suddenly nipped her finger — something she hadn't expected from her tame little chipmunk. Then he scampered off into the garden and was not seen for days.

"You couldn't keep him for ever," I consoled Sue. "It's much better that he finds his own food and runs wild with the others."

She resigned herself to the fact that Chippy would not return, and no doubt had other worries about going to boarding school for the first time.

On the final evening of our holidays, we were always taken to the cinema and then for a Chinese meal. This was intended to take our minds off our impending departure from home, which made us sisters gloomy. If the film was

Sue, nicknamed 'Skinamalinky-long-legs' by my father,
on the eve of her introduction to boarding school

a sad one, it was usually Dad who shed tears and was then cheered up by our enthusiasm for Chinese food, which we all loved, with the exception of my mother. Although she had gone out East to marry my father twenty years before, and they lived at first in the Federal Malay States, she had never learned to like Chinese, Indian or any other Asian food, and if possible never ate it. On these evenings, when we chose a profusion of dishes, she toyed with a plate of Egg Fuyong and watched us devouring with pleasure.

It had been my mother's job to prepare and pack for each of us a tin trunk with all we needed for school. Our things were colour-coded, so Jane had wash-bag, face flannels, and anything else that could be in pink, Sue had green, and I had chosen blue. Apart from our school uniforms of blue Aertex shirts and grey skirts and woollies, we could take other clothes to wear at weekends, and in my case, because I was a senior girl, for supper in the evening. All these had to be name taped and this job was done by somebody we called 'the Sewing Lady'.

The Sewing Lady, Mary, was Anglo-Indian, a term now applied to those of mixed descent, although earlier in the Raj it had been used to refer to all British persons in India. Mary was elderly, with grey hair, very thin and frail, and according to my mother, not very well off. She came once a week and, apart from sewing on name tapes, did any mending we had. My mother never wanted to tell her she did not need her any more, so if there was nothing else to do, she had her endlessly embroidering our initials on handkerchiefs, table napkins, and anything else she could think up. Every Thursday, Mary sat in the cool of our spare room and was given a good lunch and then tea. She spoke with a chi-chi accent, the rendering of English which gave her speech a lilting sing-song sound. In the later days of the Raj, this was something British parents dreaded their offspring would pick up. They went to great lengths to keep their children from acquiring it, as it was considered quite unacceptable and might indicate 'a touch of the tar-brush'; in other words, of not pure British ancestry. When I sat and talked to Mary, I learned that she was helping her daughter, a single mother, to send her granddaughter, Lisa, to school. Apparently Lisa was very bright and loved her school near her home.

Our trunks had a longer journey to school. They were far too big to be taken into the car, so they were loaded onto a bullock cart and sent to Madras Central Station, accompanied by our waterman, Munswami. I always thought it strange that cows were allowed to wander anywhere, whereas bullocks were used as work horses. I suppose, being castrated bulls, they produced neither milk nor offspring, and had to prove their usefulness somehow.

One of the visitors to our compound was a man who came with a bullock he had taught to perform. According to Ayah, this was probably done very cruelly by beating the animal, which had learned to kneel, to offer one hoof like a dog, to turn in a tight circle, and generally make a lot of noise with the bells tied to its painted horns. This brought my mother to the front verandah and she would try telling the man to go away; but he was very persistent and knew that if he waited until we children came out, we would beg for him to be allowed to give his show. It was conducted by the owner shouting loud commands and sometimes, to our dismay, using a stick.

The bullock cart drivers also used sticks, and with our trunks, had heavy loads to deliver to the station. There, Munswami arranged for them to be put on the overnight train which we would catch that evening. We would not see them again until they turned up at St. Hilda's School. As far as we knew, the train was met next morning in Coimbatore at the foot of the Hills by a lorry, which the school had arranged to transport the trunks up through the tortuous hairpin bends to Ooty. Our bedding rolls we took to the station in the boot of the car, and these were also collected by the lorry in Coimbatore.

So tin trunks, good for storing belongings insect-free, and bedding rolls, required for most train journeys, were two essential items for expatriates in India, even children, if they were going to boarding school in the Hills.

The Journey Back to School

The evening came for us three sisters to make the journey to school. It would take us about seventeen hours. We stood on the platform in Madras Central Station surrounded by porters in loin cloths and crimson shirts. The Nilgiri Express was getting up steam for its overnight run to Mettupalayam. Joseph, our driver, had got us to the station in good time for the 8 p.m. departure. Soon, after parking the car, he would come to say good-bye to his three Missies. Sue had hold of Ayah's hand and seemed to be torn between excitement and tears. Jane was already crying, as she always did on leaving home. We would be away for almost five months, although my mother would come to the Hills some time during the Hot Weather and take us out of school for weekends.

At the beginning of each term, of which there were two, the school organised a number of teachers to escort a group of children from Madras to Ootacamund. We had school mates from all over India, but they congregated in Madras and made a large group. Each train compartment was an isolated entity with its own shower and hole-in-the-floor lavatory. This is where we girls learned that it is better not to wear trousers on an Indian train because of the difficulty of keeping them off the floor while managing other necessary manoeuvres. There were no communicating corridors. The compartments slept only four or six, and there were never enough teachers to go round, so the senior girls were put in charge of the younger ones.

My father was now paying off the porters and organising the bedding rolls, which we would open as soon as the train departed. 'Better unroll Sue's for her,' I thought, wondering whether the sardines and condensed milk had been packed in my holdall. The three of us and three others were allocated to a compartment, so I realised that we would have no teacher with us. Just as well, because eating our sardines and condensed milk in the middle of the night would most certainly have been frowned on. There were hugs and kisses all round and we climbed regretfully into the train. Going back to school was always sad, though nothing compared to the dejection of being left behind in England.

Once the train started, we got ready for bed, putting on pyjamas and setting out our bedding rolls. There were three bunks at window level and three above.

"I want one upstairs," said Sue.

"No," I vetoed, "I don't want you falling out. Anyway, you can see much better from a bottom one."

For this reason, I too had commandeered a lower bunk, leaving the others to be argued over.

The train roared into the night and we slept only fitfully for there was far too much excitement when we stopped at stations. The noise and the light kept us all awake. There were families with bundles, women with innumerable children, all trying to get on the train. Sometimes, although we were travelling 1st Class in pre-booked compartments, there would be knocking on our door with passengers trying to find an empty bunk; but we were under strict instructions not to unlock our door at any time. Because the train had no corridors, the vendors ran up and down the platform shouting their wares. There was the cha-wallah wanting to sell us tea and coffee; the man selling samosas, bhajis and even biryanis; the fruit vendor who tried to tempt us with oranges and bananas. All transactions took place through the windows, but we would not let down our mesh shutters as we would not have dared to buy anything to eat in case it gave us 'Delhi Belly'. Anyway, we had our sardines and condensed milk to consume.

This was the nearest we got to the midnight feasts we'd read about in schoolgirls' stories.

As dawn broke, we packed up our bedding rolls ready for a change of trains in Coimbatore. There, a gaggle of girls and a few small boys were shepherded into the station dining room for breakfast. We ate congealed scrambled eggs and limp toast with jam, which led Jane to mutter, "I wish we were having breakfast at home. At least we might get a banana." She was always upset at going back to school and it would take her days to get over her homesickness.

Next we re-boarded the train for the short journey to Mettupalayam, which lies at the foot of the Ghats and is the railhead for the Blue Mountain Toy Train or Nilgiri Mountain Railway. The last leg of our journey would take us away from the heat of the Plains up into the cool and rarefied air of the hill station of Ootacamund; and though it was only 29 miles, it would take us almost five hours. The line was built by Swiss engineers over a hundred years ago, and finally finished in 1908. In order to reach the height of 7,350 feet, the steam train has to negotiate terrain that is rugged and rocky and includes forests and waterfalls. The little toy train, on a narrow gauge rail, has to zig-zag its way in order to conquer the gradient. Sometimes there are landslides, which curtail the service, but we never experienced these on our many journeys to and from school. There are sixteen tunnels and, as we chugged through them, the younger children always set up a shout. We passed tiny shacks at the side of the line, where ragged urchins called out to us and waved, and we waved back. We were forbidden to lean out of the wide, open windows, which was dangerous because of the narrow gorges we passed through. There were several stations along the route, but at Hill Grove, the train stopped for longer to take on water. Because the carriages had no toilets, those of us who needed to, rushed to the station facilities, usually most unpleasant and odorous. We saw many monkeys on the journey, and at stations they came to the platform hoping that passengers would give them food. By the time we reached Coonoor we needed our cardigans and were beginning to feel hungry.

Shortly before one o'clock, the little train pulled in to Ootacamund station. Generally called Ooty, and now officially known as Udhagamandalam, the town is 7,349 feet above sea level and St. Hilda's School was, and still is, on a hill above it. We were pleased to find the school bus waiting to take us up there.

We were greeted by a smiling headmistress and her dachshunds, of which she had several, and by Matron, who showed us which dormitories we had been allocated. Lunch felt long overdue and was heartily devoured. Afterwards, it was time to catch up with old friends and unpack our trunks. Little Sue seemed rather lost, and Jane and I did our best to comfort her and keep her busy, helping her to put her things away in her cupboard and the locker which stood at the end of her bed. It was the first time she had been away from our parents and we could understand her distress.

"Mum will be in Ooty in less than two months," I told her, "and the time will go very quickly."

That evening, when I went to say good night to my two sisters, I found each of them crying quietly into their pillows. It took a few days, a busy school routine, and the chatter of their schoolmates to return them to their usual cheerful selves. I was just thankful to be only a few hundred miles away from my parents, and not thousands of miles away in England.

CHAPTER ELEVEN

Dancing Class

In our white tutus and dancing pumps, we ran across the school playground clutching our hard-blocked ballet shoes. It was Wednesday afternoon and there were no lessons for the rest of the school, but some of our parents had chosen for us the extra-curricular activity of a dancing class with the fearsome Miss Symons. She was a large, middle-aged lady, who came every week with her piano playing assistant and put us through an hour-and-a-half of discomfort for body and soul. Not only were our pretty pink-beribboned ballet shoes tough on our toes, but her biting tongue reduced many of us to jelly. She was, nevertheless, a good teacher and could at times be lavish with her praise. One of her favourites was my sister Jane, who seemed able to perform her pas de chat with more grace than most of us.

There were usually ten or twelve of us, all sizes and ages, and any one of us could bear the brunt of our teacher's criticism. Despite or perhaps because of her fierce demeanour, she did manage to turn even the clumsiest of us into agile cygnets, if not elegant swans. In fact, a Ceylonese classmate went on to become a ballerina in Europe.

Apart from traditional ballet manoeuvres, we were also taught folkloric dances. I struggled to coordinate my arms and legs for the Highland Fling and enjoyed much more the Sailor's Hornpipe, while the pianist sang along with the refrain 'what do we do with a drunken sailor'.

We learned to dance the Polish Mazurka and an Irish Jig. They were a far cry from Bharat Natyam and other types of Indian dancing, which some of our Asian classmates were introduced to at home. One year, we practised for hours perfecting the Maypole Dance, which we performed around a Maypole set up in the school playground. Our fellow pupils and any of their parents in Ooty at the time came to watch us, dressed as peasants and managing, only just, not to muddle up the multi-coloured ribbons.

In 1953, Miss Symons decided to produce a Coronation play. Her dancing class pupils were to be the stars. The production was entitled, 'Freedom Within Law' and began with two children, Elizabeth and Philip, discussing History. In order to convince Elizabeth that history is more than mere battles and wars, the Spirit of History stages scenes from the past proving the foundation of England's rule to be Freedom within Law for all. The scenes covered the rules of King Alfred, King Canute, King John and King Edward lll, and were followed by the performance of ancient court dances. For these, we needed a great deal of practice.

The first two dances were the Pavane and the Galliard, representing the Early Tudor period. Two of my classmates, Durr and Dee, took part in these. To represent the Late Tudor period, Jane and her classmate, Alice, danced the Allemande, and I followed with the Coranto. As this was a solo, I found it nerve racking. For the Stuart period, eight of us were chosen to dance the Jig, followed by Jane and Alice again, doing the Bourree. We much preferred the Minuet and the Gavotte, which I performed with my classmate Ann

Livy, to cover the Georgian period. Jane and Amrita then danced the Victorian Polka, and the sequence ended with two friends of Miss Symons dancing the Waltz, Foxtrot and Tango.

While all these rehearsals were taking place, the school derzi was busy producing costumes, so that we would be attired appropriately for the decades we were representing. Trying them on was the best part of the preparations.

The play then continued with a ballet depicting the Abolition of Slavery. This involved quite a large cast with Jane, as the Spirit of Conscience, invoking Humanity to take action, resulting in Abolition of Slavery Bills passed in 1833 and 1865.

The final act was a Freedom of India ballet in which the Commonwealth of Nations, represented by Australia, Africa, Canada, Ceylon, Newfoundland and New Zealand arrive to witness the bestowal of Freedom on India. Britannia garlands India with the Garland of Freedom and India elects to remain a member of the Commonwealth.

The play took place at the Coonoor Club, and we were surprised how many people had come to see the St. Hilda's girls dancing. We managed the performance without any glaring mistakes, and the finale was greeted with enthusiastic applause, probably led by our fellow schoolmates.

AMATEURS AT THE ASSEMBLY ROOMS

"Come on, let's have a look behind your ears," said Durr, the school's head girl.

She bounced out of bed and leaned on my locker.

"I feel alright, so I expect it's OK," I answered, telling myself I had better get up.

"We ought to make sure," said Ann Livy, another classmate, who I knew was equally reluctant to tear herself away from the mattress. "Have you got a temperature, do you think?"

"I don't think so."

"What will we do if the spots come out before next Saturday? You might feel awful with it — I did," said Dee, who'd had her nose in a book since first light.

"What's worrying me," I countered, "is that I still don't know my lines."

"For heaven's sake, hurry up and learn them then," said Dee. "It's easy. I've got Jaque's part off pat already."

"It's all very well for you," said Diane from the other end of the dormitory, trying to comb the knots out of her tight fair curls. "Yours is only a bit part. I'm still not word perfect, and Anne only took over a week ago." Diane was to play Rosalind to my Orlando. Durr pushed my hair out of the way and inspected the back of my ears.

"Can you see any?" asked Christine from two beds down the dormitory.

"Nothing yet," Durr replied.

Was I or was I not going to get chicken pox? More to the point, was I going to get it before we acted *As You Like It* to the inhabitants of Ootacamund?

Shakespeare's play was one of the set books for the Senior Cambridge Exam, which I would sit and pass at the end of the year, before leaving St. Hilda's. Our headmistress had decided that it would be helpful to perform it, and had entrusted Miss Range, our games mistress and an elocution teacher, with its production. We would appear at the Assembly Rooms, Ooty's theatre and cinema. As performance day approached, almost the entire school had gone down with chicken-pox. Suzanne, who should have played the lead role, Orlando, had succumbed only a week before and, to my consternation, I was given the part.

The cast of 'As you Like It',
performed by St. Hilda's at the Assembly Rooms, Ooty

"It's lucky Diane's had chickenpox," said Yamuna, "or we'd really be up the creek. Are you sure you didn't have it when you were little?"

"My mother says I didn't," I replied.

"Well, you'd better take your script with you when we go to Government Gardens this afternoon, and we'll all take turns testing you."

That afternoon we went on a picnic to the lovely botanical Gardens that lie below Ootacamund's Government House. We walked in single file through one of the side gates and were pleased that we were there at last, because it was a long walk from St. Hilda's up on the hill. The cannas were in full bloom and the well-tended flower beds of the Gardens were ablaze with reds and yellows. We walked on now in small groups to one of our favourite picnic spots. This was a steep grassy bank, shaded at the bottom by a few trees. Miss Range blew her whistle and we all gathered round.

"We'll have tea in an hour," she said, "but if I blow two short blasts on the whistle, you are all to come back here at once."

Although the Gardens are very large, we knew that none of us would venture far. We hadn't insisted on this particular spot for our picnic for no reason. It was, after all, the best slope for a favourite game. The little ones were already at it.

"You didn't put your new ones on, did you?" asked Liela of Kalpana, one of the youngest.

"I didn't know this morning that we were coming here. Anyway, I don't care," replied Kalpana, as she dumped herself on the ground and slithered down the grassy bank at a pace.

"Oh, I can get further than that," said Liela, pulling up

her skirt and shooting right down to the trees at the bottom, ending up in a heap.

"How do you do that? Do you think it's my new knickers?" asked Kalpana, trying to see the back of them. "Have they gone awfully green?"

"Not yet," said Jeremy, the most mischievous boy in the school, having a good look while pretending nonchalantly to sharpen a stick with his penknife. "But come up here to the top again and I'll give you a push. You're bound to get further than Liela then, and your new knickers will never be the same again."

I sat under the trees with the other 'A' Form girls and watched the younger ones as they climbed again and again to the top of the slope and whizzed down on their bottoms. I heard Nurse muttering to Miss Range, who was sitting a few feet away,

"I hope to God the dhobi gets the grass stains out of those knickers."

"Well, it's no good trying to stop them," said Miss Range. "They would only wander off round the corner and use that grassy bank. I suppose it's quite harmless and keeps them amused. I just wonder what the malis think about having their lawns worn threadbare. As long as we don't get a complaint from Government House, it should be OK."

"The Governor is not in residence yet," replied Nurse, "so they won't have the whole retinue up there being officious about the state of the Gardens. As far as complaints are concerned, I should think there are more of those after they've had the huge crowds tramping through to view the displays at the Flower Show."

Trying to listen to all this was keeping me from concentrating on my lines. *As You Like It* was banished from my mind as I thought about the Ooty Flower Show. It was an annual event to which exhibits were brought from the gardens, both large and small, of local Ooty inhabitants. Many of these were elderly and had retired to the hill station because the hot climate of the Plains affected their health. Their homes were usually small cottages perched in among the nooks and crannies of the Ooty hillside. The larger, more palatial houses were the second homes of more wealthy people, who only came to Ootacamund for the Hot Weather.

The next day we clambered down the shortcut to St. Stephen's Church and lined up in two's for our walk to the Assembly Rooms. Our Head and our Deputy Headmistress were bringing the costumes down in their little car for the Dress Rehearsal. This came to an abrupt halt when the footlights fused and a plaintive voice called from the wings. "Wait, wait, I've pressed the wrong button."

We waited in vain for three minutes until we discovered that Jeremy had, by mistake, according to him, thrown the main switch in the wrong direction.

"Oh, I thought I was supposed to do that," he murmured, when the error of his ways was pointed out.

Suspecting him of just being mischievous, I cast a knowing glance at Diane.

"He'll probably have one of us breaking a leg before tomorrow," she muttered, "and I hope to God you're going to be alright, because the way you reacted when I forgot my lines isn't going to see us through our gala performance."

The way I was feeling, I prayed that I would make the gala performance.

"What's the matter?" asked Durr that evening, as I climbed into bed with a sigh. "Do you think you've got it yet?"

"I don't know," I replied, "but I do feel a bit feverish."

Next morning we had an inspection.

"Those spots could be them," said Dee. "They look like the ones I had."

"No point worrying about it now," I replied. I finished polishing my shoes and pulled the blanket up over my bed, hoping that Matron would not notice that I hadn't stripped it today.

It was performance day, and the cast went downtown in the school bus. I skulked in a dark corner of the changing room, dreading the moment I would have to appear before our make-up artiste/producer.

"She's bound to notice," said Ann Livy. "She may be only our Games Mistress, but she isn't that stupid that she won't see the ones that have come out now."

I felt sick with stage fright and hot with fever.

"I think I can do my own make up, Miss Range," I ventured.

"Oh no you don't," she countered and propelled me over to the make up chair.

I cringed under the bright light, and hoped to God she wouldn't knock the heads off my spots and scar me for life.

"Now look," she said, "I'm going to listen out for you especially, because I think you may need prompting." She spread the grease paint carefully around the largest spot on my right temple. "I know you're not feeling too good, but if you think you're going to faint, make a sign with your hand behind your back, and I'll get David to bring the curtain down."

I knew by the way she looked at me that she had guessed, and I thank her to this day that I am not more scarred by chicken-pox than I needed to be. I managed to get through the performance. Nobody forgot her lines, and David had to wait for all the applause to end before he could ring down the curtain. I was only pleased that it was a Friday evening, and I could slink home to my mother, who was up from the Plains, and go to bed for the weekend.

THE CLUB SCENE

Apart from parties in their homes, much of an expatriate's social life in India centred around the Clubs. In Madras, there were several, all of which had some facilities for sports. The Madras Club, which was the most exclusive of them all, had three different homes in the time that I knew it. The first one had an indoor swimming pool and was where I learned to swim. Apparently, when I was two and before I had mastered the skill, I jumped into the water without warning and had to be fished out. The pool had ropes hanging from the ceiling, and people could swing out across the water from a high diving board. A couple of years later, I remember the excitement of being held in my father's arms as he swung and let go of the rope, and we descended with a huge splash into the deep end.

The Club's second home was on Mount Road, and there I learned to dance Scottish reels at a session that was held every Monday evening. These I was allowed to attend as a club member's offspring, and was warned to be on my best behaviour. It struck me that this was a very sedate place, where the members were mostly burra- sahibs and their wives.

The Madras Club's final and present home are the premises at Adyar, which was once the Adyar Club. That Club was much less staid and had great facilities for children including swings, seesaws and a sand pit, as well as a large aviary, where we were fascinated by the variety of colourful birds. The Adyar Club's Christmas party for members' children was a joyous affair. We went in our organdie party frocks and buttoned shoes with little white socks. There was a merry-go-round set on the large lawn, which stretched from the Clubhouse down to the Adyar River, and sometimes Father Christmas arrived by boat to deliver his presents. Other years, he came on horseback, or in a decorated jeep. He led us across the wide terrace and into the ballroom, where presents were piled around the decorated Casuarina tree, and we waited in eager anticipation for him to hand a labelled gift to each child.

The Clubhouse is an imposing white building with high-ceilinged rooms and many doors opening out to verandahs around it. The entrance is particularly impressive with steps leading from the vast elephant porch to the black and white floor of the portico held up by huge pillars. There was once a lot of land around it, which included a golf course, with browns not greens, tennis courts and beautifully tended flowerbeds. At that time there was not yet the swimming pool, which now exists.

There were also other buildings in the grounds, which were apartments where bachelor members could live. They were usually the older members because the younger bachelors tended to live in a chummery — a house shared by a number of them. My first home, Wallace Gardens, had a chummery on the floor above us and its high-spirited inhabitants, who attended my christening, are said to have rolled my Aunt Mary up in a carpet and carried her off upstairs to continue the party. I still have the silver christening mug they gave me, engraved with all their signatures.

High spirits, fuelled by beer, particularly after rugger practice at the Gymkhana Club, led to numerous incidents frowned upon by older members. It was not thought appropriate to ride a horse on to the dance floor, or to let loose through the skylights the Club's entire stock of toilet rolls. The instigators were hauled up before the Committee and reprimanded. I never heard whether the young man, who streaked naked through the astonished memsahibs seated in the Club lounge, was allowed to remain a member.

In Madras, there was a band of older bachelors, or men whose wives had given up on India and taken their children to school in Britain, who called themselves 'The Derelicts'. In January every year, they held a splendid white-tie Ball, which was the highlight of the Cold Weather season. An invitation to this was much coveted. The year I turned seventeen I received the much-prized invitation. Admittedly, it was only because 'Uncle' Charles, who was a good friend of my parents, knew that I loved dancing and thought that I might like to attend. I was pleased and excited at being asked.

My mother and I began looking in magazines and pattern books for a dress that MK, our derzi, could copy. We decided on a strapless number with a full skirt and three tiers of frill around the back and sides, and then we went looking for material. I thought about black.

"No" said my mother, "you're much too young for black, and anyway I'm wearing my black dress with tiered pleats."

The obliging man in Chellaram's pulled out bolt after bolt of silks, satins and taffetas. Finally I made my choice — an ice green taffeta that would make the skirt rustle as I moved. I smiled to myself because I remembered sitting in the church at Fort St. George when I was twelve, and deciding that my first long dress would be green. Strapless bras were difficult to obtain in Madras in those days, and MK did a skilful job boning the bodice of my dress so that everything stayed in place. I was delighted with his creation.

Finally the big day arrived. Despite my feelings of on-coming maturity, I was glad to have my Ayah there when I dressed for the evening. She had laid out my shoes and the little silver bag my mother was lending me, and now she helped me do up my dress, just as she had over all the years. She would not be there always, but she has certainly stayed in my thoughts my whole life long.

I went to the sitting room, where my parents were having photographs taken so that I would remember this

My mother, father and myself, ready for the Derelicts Ball held at
the Adyar Club

as a very special occasion. My father had ordered orchids for Mum and me to pin to our dresses.

"Anne, I hope you will have the first dance with me," he said.

Then we were ready to leave for the Adyar Club.

The Club's premises were bedecked with flowers. The ballroom, in particular, looked enchanting with garlands of bougainvillaea hanging from the ceiling. A lavish buffet was laid out in another room, and I felt less shy as my dance card began to fill up. Sympathetic 'Uncles' were writing in their names for the whole evening's programme. Much to my satisfaction, I ended up not sitting out a single dance and thoroughly enjoyed myself. It was certainly a night to remember, and I felt that I was emerging into adulthood from the exceedingly happy and fascinating childhood I had spent in India.

Lightning Source UK Ltd.
Milton Keynes UK
UKRC01n2154180118
316410UK00001BA/8